Dedicated to my father, Ken Wattman, who instructed my brilliant brother, George, and me to "enjoy your life," and to Brian Muno who helps me do so.

MARY LOU WATTMAN

Dedicated to my wife, Diane, who is battling cancer as this book goes to print.

And, to my parents, Don and Mary Ann, who have been the greatest influence on my understanding of leadership, and are the most ardent supporters of the research we are conducting to advance the subjects covered in this book.

DON TRONE

This is the logo of 3ethos, which represents the link between leadership, stewardship and governance.

Table of Contents

Why We Wrote *LeaderMetrics*® 6

Our Infographics 8

The LeaderMetrics® Wheel 11

Ethos – The Katrina Story 12

Indigenous Wisdom 18

The Power of the Tripartite 19

The LeaderMetrics® Framework 20

    Applied LeaderMetrics: *Shayna's Story* 27

    Infographic for the Michigan Medical Model 33

Leadership 34

    Applied LeaderMetrics: *Man Overboard* .55

    Infographic for Rear Admiral Steve Branham, USCG (Retired) 61

Stewardship 62

    Applied LeaderMetrics: *Where Everything Matters* 87

    Infographic for Jim Lumberg 99

Governance 100

    Applied LeaderMetrics: *Risky Business* 123

    Infographic for William (Bill) Zachry 131

Assessing Your Strengths and Weaknesses .132

    Applied LeaderMetrics: *Master of the Sword* 147

    Infographic for Brigadier General Maureen LeBoeuf,
    U.S. Army (Retired) 155

Parting Praxes 156

    Applied LeaderMetrics: *Taking Comfort in Leading from the Front* . . .167

    Infographic for William F. (Bill) Murdy 177

The 3ethos Challenge Coin 178

About the GFS® Designation 179

LeaderMetrics® Self-assessment Instrument 182

About "Applied LeaderMetrics"

At the end of each major section of the book, in a section called "Applied LeaderMetrics," we are going to share a wonderfully true narrative which illustrates the concept of a framework that integrates leadership, stewardship and governance.

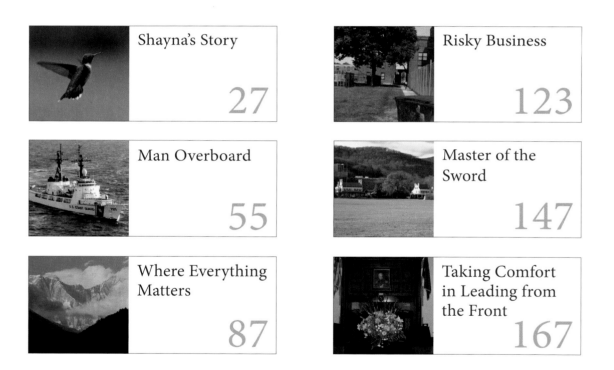

Shayna's Story 27	Risky Business 123
Man Overboard 55	Master of the Sword 147
Where Everything Matters 87	Taking Comfort in Leading from the Front 167

LeaderMetrics
Self-assessment Instrument

In the back of this book is a self-assessment instrument which is based on the LeaderMetrics® framework, and is divided into three sections – Leadership, Stewardship and Governance. By taking the assessment you can more easily determine your strengths and weaknesses.

You can take the assessment now, to help you familiarize yourself with the topics which we will be covering; or later, to assess your comprehension of the material.

This instrument is not scored – there is no such thing as passing or failing. In fact, we would expect, for the majority of statements, you will be indicating that it is a strength – a "1" or a "2."

The instrument's greatest value is identifying your weaknesses – the statements where you give yourself a "3" or a "4." If by reading this book you can begin to focus on even one of your weaknesses, then, as authors, we will have accomplished one of our primary objectives.

Why We Wrote *LeaderMetrics*

This is the first book to integrate the three subjects of leadership, stewardship and governance. There are tens of thousands of books on leadership; nearly an equal number on governance, decision-making and project management; and, a handful on stewardship. However, this is the first to link all three topics.

⚐ LeaderMetrics® is a new body of research which provides for a hierarchical framework to facilitate the development and evaluation of a key decision-maker serving in a critical leadership role.

⚐ You should find *LeaderMetrics* to be an invaluable desktop reference if you are serving as an advisor, consultant, trustee, director, investment committee member, or officer. And, you should also find the book to be applicable whether you work for a corporation, not-for-profit, government entity or the military.

⚐ More importantly, we also intend for *LeaderMetrics* to be a guide and a reminder that leadership carries a moral and ethical responsibility to be of service to others.

Leadership is your single most important point of differentiation, and chances are you are underestimating the impact your leadership has on others. There is an energy which is generated from authentic leadership, and you are the steward of that power. There is no better way to lead than to do so for the benefit of others.

The key to your success will be your
Ability to inspire and Capacity to serve.

You will be known by your
Character, Competence and Courage;
and, for the
Purpose, Passion and Process
you project when protecting the long-term interests of others.

Mary Lou Wattman and Don Trone
Summer of 2014

*Hometown
Chadds Ford, PA*

*North Carolina State University
B.A. Economics
and Business Management*

P&G

Mary Lou Wattman, GFS®
Co-founder
3ethos

Founder and CEO
1920West

*Northwestern University
MBA – Marketing and
Organizational Behavior*

*Professional Behaviors Analyst
Professional Motivators Analyst*

seven
*Led 200 people in
media and printing
company*

*Traveled the world and
consulted to Fortune 500
companies and start-ups.*

*COO of a not-for-profit
organization*

8

Hometown
West Chester, PA

1973 – 1977
USCG Academy

1977 – 1987
U.S. Coast Guard

Donald B. Trone, GFS®
Founder and CEO
3ethos

2011   *2008*   *2003*

RAYMOND JAMES®
1987 – 1989

SEI
1988 – 1991

3ethos®
2008 – Present
Founder and CEO

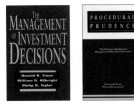

1995   *1989*

THE AMERICAN COLLEGE OF FINANCIAL SERVICES
1987 – 1989
M.S.

2007 – 2009
First Director

PITTSBURGH
THEOLOGICAL
SEMINARY
2001 – 2005
Graduate Studies

1998 – 2007
Founder and CEO

Callan
1991 – 1998
Executive Vice President

The Need for LeaderMetrics®

Only one in every three workers feel they are engaged and inspired by the work they are doing. The number one reason given for disengagement is poor leadership. The results are even more discouraging when you consider that disengaged employees are less productive, less innovative, produce more customer complaints, have more on-the-job accidents, and have higher absenteeism. Consider the following:

Gallop (gallop.com) in its recent survey on employee engagement found that in the U.S. only 30% of employees feel they are engaged at work; 52% are not engaged, and 18% are actively disengaged.

LRN (lrn.com) conducts an annual survey to measure how governance, culture and leadership influence employee behavior. The results of its most recent survey:

- 3% of employees believe they work for an organization which is based on trust, shared values and principles.

- 54% believe they work for an organization which is rules-based and motivated by individual self-interests.

- 43% believe they are being subjected to coercive, autocratic authority.

Right Management (right.com), a subsidiary of Manpower Group, surveyed American workers and found that:

- 19% are satisfied with their jobs
- 16% are somewhat satisfied
- 21% are somewhat unsatisfied
- 44% are unsatisfied

The LeaderMetrics® Wheel

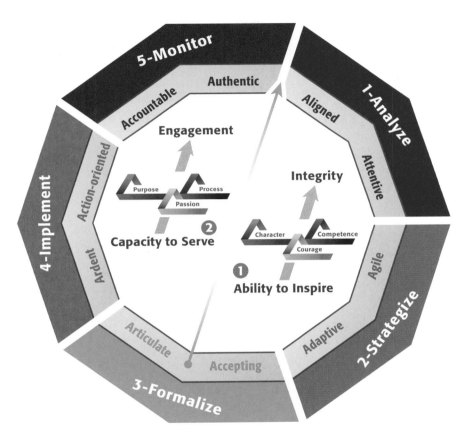

Inner ring
2 Leadership Tenets
Leadership is your sense of **Purpose** – *if missing, followers will feel anxious.*

Middle ring
10 Stewardship Attributes
Stewardship is your **Passion** – *if missing, followers will disengage.*

Outer ring
5 Governance Steps
Governance is your **Process** – *if missing, followers will feel confused.*

Throughout the book we are going to be referencing the LeaderMetrics® Wheel. In designing this framework, we have tried our best to strike a balance between simplicity and inclusiveness. At first, it may appear to be complex, but give it some time and you'll discover that it is a relatively simple framework to master.

Ethos – The Katrina Story

Ethos (ē'thos) n. The distinguishing leadership behaviors, core values and decision-making process of a person, group, or institution.

On August 29, 2005, Hurricane Katrina slammed into New Orleans. Over the next nine days, U.S. Coast Guard forces, under the leadership of Rear Admiral Robert F. Duncan, rescued more than 24,500 people. To put this heroic response into perspective, the Coast Guard rescues an average of 5,500 people each year, worldwide.

Photo courtesy of Claire Carroll

You really can't just show up and say, 'We're going to do a really big hurricane response here,' and start that work on Sunday before the storm on Monday. This sort of thing has to be put in place, rehearsed, and practiced. And everyone has to have a shared vision of how you would bring assets in to provide relief across a spectrum that's really historic.

Rear Admiral Robert F. Duncan, USCG
Commander, Eighth Coast Guard District

Ethos – The Katrina Story

On September 9, 2005, President George Bush relieved Michael Brown as the Director of the Federal Emergency Management Agency and replaced him with Vice Admiral Thad Allen. [Admiral Allen would later go on to become the 23rd Commandant of the U.S. Coast Guard.]

The Coast Guard was faced with the same crisis as every other government agency, but it outperformed them all. How, and why?

As natural and manmade disasters increase in frequency and intensity we need leaders who can confront complexity, challenge the status quo, and work across boundaries to create unity of effort. One of the Coast Guard's Principles of Operations is the principle of on scene initiative. You don't wait for a directive from higher authority to act when the situation demands it. Our aircrews from Air Station New Orleans understood this and acted on it, flying in marginal conditions as soon as possible following Katrina's landfall.

Vice Admiral Thad Allen, USCG
Chief of Staff, U.S. Coast Guard

In 2007, Don accepted an offer to become the first Director of the Institute for Leadership at the U.S. Coast Guard Academy. During his time at the Institute one of the pet projects of the staff was to try to find a concise answer to the question: **"Why was the Coast Guard so successful in its response to Katrina?"**

About nine months into the research they came across the ancient Greek word "ethos." They knew instantly it was the answer they'd been looking for — **the Coast Guard has a well-defined ethos.** No matter where you sample the Coast Guard's inner core, you find a consistency in the leadership behaviors, core values and decision-making process of the organization. The differences between a good and great leader, even between a good and a great organization, can be explained in terms of a well-defined ethos.

The staff then set about to find a model which would replicate an ethos — a framework which would enable researchers to link leadership behaviors, core values, and a decision-making process. Much to their disappointment, they couldn't find one. It was then that Don decided to begin the work which would eventually lead to the formation of the company 3ethos (3ethos.com), and the writing of this book.

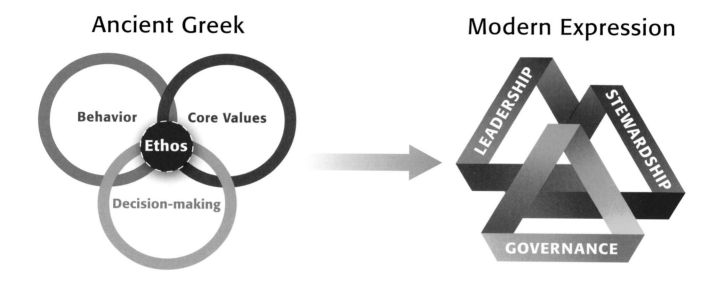

Ancient Greek

- Behavior
- Core Values
- Ethos
- Decision-making

Modern Expression

- LEADERSHIP
- STEWARDSHIP
- GOVERNANCE

The modern expression of ethos is the link between leadership, stewardship and governance – the focus of this book. We will take an integrated approach to define a process which binds these three terms, and outline the requisites which will make your role and responsibilities as a leader, steward and decision-maker authentic and aligned.

We're not alone in our discovery – "ethos" is fast becoming the executive power word. For years organizations have mounted mission and vision statements on their walls only to discover that during the recent economic crisis such statements proved to be ineffective rallying points.

Ethos can't be faked, copied or plagiarized, and no two people or organizations have the same ethos. Your personal ethos will be as unique as your fingerprints and your signature. You will be known by your ethos, whether or not you take the time to define it. If you are committed to defining your ethos, this book will help you through the process.

The currency of mission, vision, and values statements has been devalued, their indiscriminate use and homogeneity rendering them feeble, uninspiring and indistinguishable from everyone else's.

Lance Secretan

Indigenous Wisdom

In 2008, we published the handbook **The Management of American Indian Investment Decisions**. In doing the research for the book we discovered a number of indigenous wisdom quotes, which we believe do a wonderful job of illuminating the concepts of leadership, stewardship and governance.

Whenever you see the medicine wheel — which depicts our 5-Step Governance process in indigenous symbols — it will be used to highlight a quote which we believe illuminates a critical theme associated with each section. As an example, this is one of our favorite quotes, which sets the right tone for the book:

The public position of the Indian has always been entirely dependent upon our private virtue. We are never permitted to forget that we do not live for ourselves alone, but for our tribe and clan. Every child, from the first days of learning, is a public servant in training.

Ohiyesa (Charles Eastman), Santee

The Power of the Tripartite

The brain finds it relatively easy to grasp three things, but becomes challenged when it is tasked to comprehend four. Three represents the simplest means of defining a solid object – length, height and width; and, the triangle is the simplest geometric expression of an enclosed area. And throughout the world, most spiritual teachings also incorporate the power of three.

Most of the models we use in this book consist of three parts:

Classical expression of ethos: **Behavior, Core values and Decision-making**

Modern expression of ethos: **Leadership, Stewardship and Governance**

3ethos motto: **Moral, Ethical and Prudent Decision-making**

Ability to inspire: **Character, Competence and Courage**

Capacity to serve: **Purpose, Passion and Process**

In turn, the 3ethos corporate logo is based on a tripartite – the interlocking triangles represent the balanced links or continuum between leadership, stewardship and governance.

The LeaderMetrics® Framework

Leadership is your sense of **Purpose** – your response to a higher calling. Your success as a leader will depend upon your ability to inspire and capacity to serve others. If leadership is missing, your followers will feel anxious.

Stewardship is your **Passion** – it is your discipline and commitment to judge wisely and objectively in order to protect the long-term interests of others. If stewardship is missing, your followers will disengage.

Governance is your **Process** – the dimensions of your procedurally prudent decision-making framework. If governance is missing, your followers will feel confused.

LeaderMetrics® is a new body of research which provides for a hierarchical framework that integrates leadership, stewardship and governance. This approach enables us to use the one LeaderMetrics® framework to support multiple professional standards of care:

⚘ Fiduciary standard for trustees, investment committee members and financial advisors;

⚘ Governance standard for directors of boards;

⚘ Project management standard for staff;

⚘ Global wealth management and best practices standard for family offices, financial advisors, financial planners, brokers and trust officers; and

⚘ Coaching, mentoring and performance evaluation standard.

In turn, there are a number of benefits associated with the framework:

⚘ Guides consistent decision-making, which facilitates communication and delegation.

⚘ Provides for a simple decision-making process, which is a key success factor when operating in a complex and dynamic environment.

⚘ Helps coaches, mentors and performance evaluators to uncover procedural and behavioral risks of decision-makers.

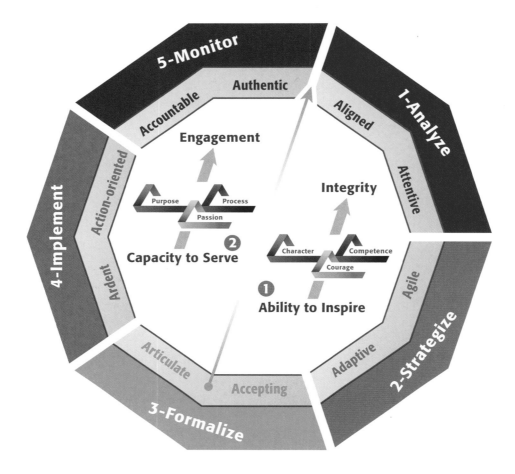

Our LeaderMetrics® Wheel consists of three rings:

The inner ring represents the 2 Leadership Tenets

The middle ring represents the 10 Stewardship Attributes

The outer ring represents the 5 Governance Steps

Leadership is Exhilarating – Governance is Exhausting

The LeaderMetrics® Wheel also is intended to model a cross-section of the brain to show where emotions associated with leadership and stewardship are processed (the inner two rings) versus complex communications and analytics (the outer ring).

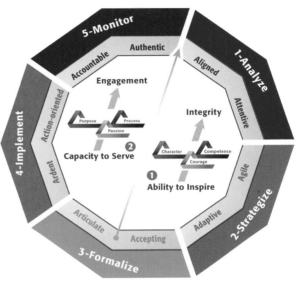

We learned about the relationship of the brain function and leadership while conducting fiduciary training in the financial services industry. After spending years trying to teach financial advisors and trustees what it means to be an investment fiduciary, we began to look for a better approach. No matter how positive we tried to make the training experience, the outcome was always the same – we scared the living daylights out of folks. Rather than feeling good about the work they were doing, they walked away feeling alarmed and concerned about their personal liability and responsibility.

However, what we did notice is that the people who wanted to become better fiduciaries also seemed to possess certain leadership characteristics. It was this observation which sent us on the quest to see if there was a link between being a great decision-maker and being a great leader.

We now know that there are physiological reasons why leadership is exhilarating and governance is exhausting – one is related to the chemicals which are released in your body, and the other to the structure of your brain. According to research at numerous universities and popularized by Simon Sinek:

⚠ When you are involved in a trusting relationship and you feel safe and secure – which should be the case when you're serving in a leadership role – the chemical oxytocin is released.

⚠ In contrast, when you are engaged in analytical decision-making – particularly when you are dealing with complex legal, financial and regulatory matters – then the chemical cortisol is released. Cortisol is an inhibitor to the creation of oxytocin.

⚠ When you are processing emotions – such as passion, trust, loyalty and a sense of security – you are using the limbic portion of your brain, which is located below and to the center of the neocortex. In order to build trust and loyalty with another person, in order to make a person feel safe and secure, you need to be able to appeal to the limbic portion of their brain – you need to touch their soul.

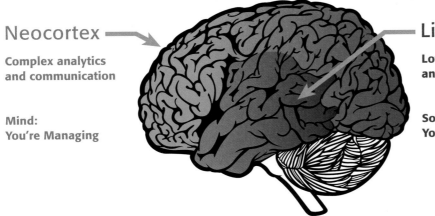

Neocortex

Complex analytics and communication

Mind: You're Managing

Limbic

Love, passion, trust and a sense of security

Soul: You're Leading

⚠ When you are processing complex analytics and communications you are using the neocortex portion of your brain, often referred to as your grey matter. The neocortex is the outer ring of the brain.

So, when we were scaring the living daylights out of advisors, directors and trustees by telling them about the personal liability they faced as a fiduciary, there was no way these same individuals were going to feel like bonding with us. Trying to build a trusting and lasting relationship with someone based on governance alone is not likely to work. Instead, you have to learn how to become a more effective leader and steward.

TRUST○METER

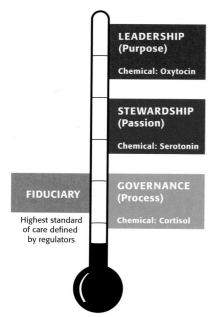

LEADERSHIP
(Purpose)

Chemical: Oxytocin

STEWARDSHIP
(Passion)

Chemical: Serotonin

FIDUCIARY

Highest standard
of care defined
by regulators

GOVERNANCE
(Process)

Chemical: Cortisol

Imagine if we could build a TrustOmeter – a trust thermometer – to take the temperature of a person or organization. We would immediately know how much trust we could put into a relationship.

If there was such a thing as a TrustOmeter, at the base (lowest temperature) would be Governance. Most organizations can point to policies and procedures manuals to demonstrate that they have good governance. On the other hand, many organizations are so hemmed in by their rules and regulations they can't register a temperature any higher than Governance.

Above Governance is Stewardship. The additional heat that raises the temperature comes from passion. Being a good steward means being passionate about the work you are doing and the people you serve.

For advisors, consultants, trustees and directors we have positioned a "Fiduciary" standard on the TrustOmeter to show its "temperature" relative to Governance and Stewardship. A fiduciary is required to demonstrate procedural prudence (details of the decision-making process) and that decisions are being made in the best interests of clients, shareholders or beneficiaries. Therefore, a fiduciary standard would fall between Governance and Stewardship. A fiduciary standard often is referred to as the highest standard defined by law – which it is. However, the operative words are, *"by law."* Keep in mind that regulatory standards (such as fiduciary) are intended to merely define the *minimum* standard of care which must be met in order for a party to be in compliance. As we will demonstrate in this book, Stewardship and Leadership actually define higher standards of care.

Shayna's Story

Whenever a hummingbird appears Shayna's parents think of her.

Shayna's Story

Shayna was eighteen months old when she died. The attending pediatric cardiologist was at fault and has admitted the same to the family. This also is a story about Shayna's father, James, and how his courage and character were strengthened by the processing of his grief.

Losing a child tests one's courage and character like few other experiences. An avalanche of emotions and questions arise regardless of the circumstances. Doctor error, miscommunication, and negligence contributed to an unbearable horror which would rattle the core of anyone.

Six weeks after Shayna's death, James received an invitation to attend a leadership boot camp for investment stewards at West Point, NY. Though still in grief, he decided to go to help himself reconnect with work. He did not expect to make a connection between being a better investment steward and being a better leader of his family.

Shayna's Story

During the course of the training, James began to see how the decision-making framework being taught in class could be used to help him and his wife gain a better understanding of what went wrong during Shayna's surgery. What protocol (decision-making framework) were the doctors and nurses supposed to follow? Did they follow that protocol, or did they deviate? Where were the shortfalls and omissions? James also began to see the framework as a source of courage – a guide which he could use if he were ever given the opportunity to talk to the doctor who had erred.

To the doctor's credit, James did have the opportunity to meet face to face with him, and as planned, James used the decision-making framework from class to keep him grounded and centered on what otherwise would have been a highly charged and emotional encounter. They discussed how very differently Shayna's body reacted to the same operation which had been performed on her twin sister just six weeks earlier. The doctor admitted that he "underappreciated" Shayna's unique health situation and the associated risks.

James believes that the attending medical team set out to do their best the day Shayna died, and that his doctor is genuinely remorseful. But at the same time, James felt he needed to do more. Shayna deserved more.

James has since reached out and joined other thought leaders in the medical community who are advocating for greater disclosure and transparency of hospital and physician error. Initial studies suggest that hospitals which publically disclose information about medical errors actually experience an improvement in patient care, an improvement in patient satisfaction, and a decrease in litigation costs. James told us,

"Full disclosure and transparency are actually a hospital's best defense; not the legal jiujitsu of the 'risk management' department."

Three months after James attended his training program at West Point he sent an email to Don:

"The leadership and stewardship aspects of the boot camp resonated with me. I was reminded that I am the leader and steward of my clients' financial lives, and I am REALLY a leader AND steward of my family as we work on our 'new normal' (life without Shayna). What we do as leaders and stewards for our clients and family is invaluable and it should never be discounted; it has real life ramifications. In the medical profession, NOT being a leader and steward can have lethal consequences."

Authors' Postscript:

James has became an active member of the medical transparency movement, known as the *Michigan Model* – see infographic on the next page. The movement has had a profound impact on improving healthcare and reducing the costs (financial and emotional) of medical malpractice.

The Michigan Model: Medical Malpractice and Patient Safety at UMHS

"Apologize and learn when we're wrong; explain and vigorously defend when we're right; and, view court as a last resort."

1988 – Albert Wu, MD publishes first study on patient safety and honesty

1994 – Lucian Leape, MD publishes, "Error in Medicine"

1997 – formation of National Patient Safety Foundation

"We have learned that when you act ethically, you tend to pull everyone up too."

Rick Boothman

1999 – Steve S. Kraman, MD pioneers proactive and principled claims management at the VA

University of Michigan Health System

2013 UMHS lawsuits drop 67%

1999 – passage of Healthcare Research and Quality Act

2013 Shayna dies at "defend and deny" non transparent hospital

2007 – formation of the NPSF Lucian Leape Institute

University of Michigan Health System

2001 UMHS adopts transparency policy

Leadership is your sense of Purpose – your response to a higher calling.

Your success as a leader will depend upon your ability to inspire and capacity to serve others.

If leadership is missing, your followers will feel anxious.

Leadership

Think back to the people who have had a positive, significant impact on your life – the teachers, spiritual advisors, coaches, bosses or mentors. What did they all have in common?

The common traits likely include that they inspired and engaged you. They expected a lot from you and knew you had worth, talent and promise.

Every worthwhile endeavor has a leadership component. Even nature will not allow a vacuum. Consider the pride, the flock, the school and the herd. From our years of experience, we have found that the simplest and most inclusive definition of leadership is *the ability to inspire and the capacity to serve*. It's important to note that you must have both.

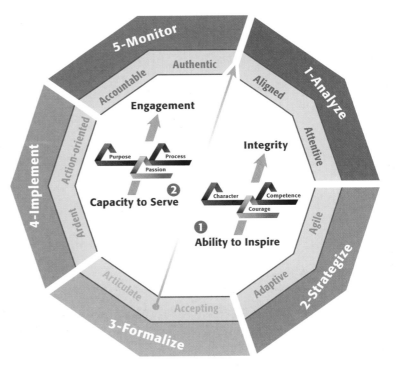

Leadership

You may be inspiring, but if you can't engage or be of service to others, then you're not a leader. You may be able to serve and engage others, but if you're not inspiring, then you're not leading. For example, professional basketball or football players may have tremendous talent and be inspiring in a charismatic sense. But if they do not serve others, or serve as positive role models, then they are not leaders.

The Ability to Inspire

We credit Lance Secretan, noted speaker and author, as the source for our writing about inspiration, particularly for highlighting the differences between inspiration and motivation. As Lance defines it, motivation almost always involves negative manipulation.

Leadership is the ability to inspire others.

What does it take to be an inspiring leader?

inspire

i integrity
n nurturing-spirit
s service-orientation
p professionalism
i intelligence
r respect for others
e effectiveness

Motivation is bribery, exploitation, manipulation and control. I want to make my targets; therefore, I will bribe you to make your targets so that when you meet them, I will meet mine. It is an act of selfishness and greed.

Lance Secretan
(Secretan.com)

If you want to inspire others – to be regarded as a leader – you must be known as a person of integrity. The tripartite which defines integrity is **Character**, **Competence** and **Courage**. As with ethos, the three components must be a continuum, be in balance with one another. A shortfall in any one of the three areas will have a negative impact on one's integrity and one's ability to lead.

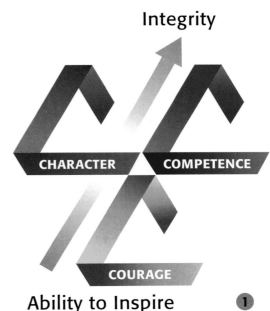

- A person who is competent and courageous but lacks character (integrity) is an ideal candidate for organized crime, but little else. Character is what informs us about right and wrong. When we lack character we may use our knowledge and courage to serve our own self-interests.

- A person who has character and is competent but lacks courage should never be put in a key decision-making role. Courage is what gives us the confidence to be decisive and to speak up when we witness wrong-doing.

- A person who has character and is courageous but lacks competence makes a great follower, but a poor leader. Competence provides us the skills to analyze, discover and prioritize.

Leadership

Integrity

People often use the words "honesty" and "integrity" interchangeably. We suggest that integrity requires more than merely being honest. A person of integrity needs to be both honest and courageous. There are a lot of people in the world who can say that they do not lie, cheat or steal – who can claim to be honest. But that does not mean they have integrity and have the courage to speak up when they witness the dishonest acts of others.

In looking for someone to hire, you look for three qualities: integrity, intelligence, and energy. But the most important is integrity, because if they don't have that, the other two qualities, intelligence and energy, are going to kill you.

Warren Buffet,
The Tao of Warren Buffet

Courage is rightly esteemed the first of human qualities... because it is the quality which guarantees all others.

Winston Churchill

Courage, as with all aspects of leadership, takes considerable effort and must be developed. Your ability to be courageous is directly correlated to the strength and depth of your principles and values. Selfish or morally weak individuals rarely have the capacity to be courageous and lead with integrity.

We use the image of an iceberg to illustrate character and competence. We witness a person's competence by their achievements and capabilities, but a person's true character remains below the surface until revealed through their behavior.

What character and competence have in common is that they both need to be nurtured and strengthened through courageous determination.

Integrity without knowledge is weak and useless, and knowledge without integrity is dangerous and dreadful.

Samuel Johnson,
The History of Rasselas, Prince of Abissinia

Leadership

The true Indian sets no price upon either his property or his labor. His generosity is limited only by his strength and ability. He regards it as an honor to be selected for a difficult or dangerous service, and would think it shameful to ask for any reward, saying rather: "Let the person I serve express thanks according to his own bringing up and his sense of honor."

Charles Alexander Eastman, Santee Lakota

Responding to Ethical Dilemmas

As a former military pilot, I spent hundreds of hours in simulators and on training flights practicing emergency procedures – honing a defined decision-making framework. We learned that during a time of extreme duress you cannot rise above a level to which you have not been trained. In my case, I piloted three severely crippled helicopters back to safe landings. I credit our survival to the great flight instructors who made me practice and simulate a response to every conceivable emergency procedure.

– Don Trone

You too need to simulate, anticipate and predict how you're going to act when faced with moral and ethical decisions. This requires a defined system and set of principles. During a time of duress – when confronted with an ethical dilemma – you are far more likely to make the right decision when you base that decision on a pre-defined framework.

The best information we have seen on moral and ethical decision-making is Dan Ariely's book, ***The (Honest) Truth About Dishonesty***. Dan writes about how even honest people have the capacity to rationalize their participation in certain dishonest acts. ***They cheat up to the point at which they can still believe in their own virtue.*** There are a number of tragic examples of once inspiring individuals who mistakenly thought integrity was situational – that they could act one way in public, and another in private.

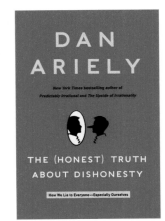

Other Points of Inspiration

⚎ Words like "trust" "honor" and "integrity" show up on everyone's list of leadership attributes. Such words, however, take on greater meaning when they are used within the context of a framework which links leadership, stewardship and governance.

⚎ Being ethical is more than merely following laws and regulations. There is much which passes as legal which is highly unethical.

⚎ Effective leadership requires resilience – the cross between having empathy and having a thick skin.

⚎ Only ethical behavior can fuel trust.

⚎ The real foundation of great leadership is character, not charisma.
   Rick Warren (pastors.com)

⚎ Reputation is based on past experiences; trust is a forward facing metric.
   Paraphrased from the Edelman Trust Barometer (Edelman.com)

⚎ To paraphrase the famous theologian, Bill Hybels – *people join organizations because of the leaders – they leave because of the managers.*

⚎ Decisions are more readily followed and supported if there is transparency in the leader's decision-making process.

Leadership

Integrity

A related phenomenon is that social forces and peer pressure can easily sway one's personal integrity: ***Everyone else is doing it, why shouldn't I?*** We have seen firsthand, people we thought were honest cower under a boardroom table at the first specter of litigation or at the prospect of losing their job. There also are those who believe that since they've never broken a law they must be ethical. We disagree; many perfectly legal actions can still be deeply unethical.

Whatever the circumstances, great leaders anticipate problems and have a framework for managing and responding to emergencies, particularly those of a moral or ethical nature. They practice and exercise their framework daily, for rarely does one receive advance notice that, today, he or she is going to be faced with an ethical dilemma. And rarer still is the person who is given time to take a break from an ethical dilemma in order to read up on emergency procedures.

Leadership

Our second leadership tenet is Engagement. You cannot lead a board, committee or team if members are not engaged.

The tripartite for Engagement is the continuum, or balance, between **Purpose**, **Passion** and **Process**. Later in the book, we are going to talk more about Passion in the Stewardship section, and Process in the Governance section.

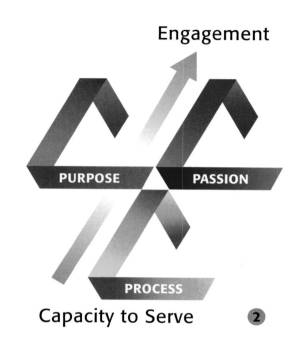

The secret of getting ahead is getting started. The secret of getting started is breaking your complex, overwhelming tasks into small manageable tasks, and then starting on the first one.

Mark Twain

Great leadership usually starts with a willing heart, a positive attitude, and a desire to make a difference.

Mac Anderson

- If you have a purpose and are passionate about what you do but you lack a process, you will waste people's time.

- If you are passionate and have a process but you lack a sense of purpose, you will be like a flare that burns brightly for a short period of time and then flames out.

- If you have a sense of purpose and process but you lack passion, you will have a difficult time leading.

> *I don't know what your destiny will be, but one thing I know: The ones among you who will be really happy are those who have sought and found how to serve.*
>
> *Albert Schweitzer*

> *To be successful, the thing to do is fall in love with your work.*
>
> *Sister Mary Lauretta*

Leadership

Purpose is your response to a higher calling. You got your first glimpse of purpose when your first-grade teacher asked you to draw a picture of what you want to become when you grow up. Chances are you drew a selfless servant – a nurse, doctor, police officer or fire fighter. Life has probably moved you off that initial calling, but to be engaging, to be inspiring, you need to project a purpose which is intended **to put the interests of others first**.

Purpose ties back to the first leadership tenet – your ability to inspire. To be engaged, people need to feel that they have a role in a big dream. Just doing a job and maintaining the status quo is not inspiring and doesn't define a sense of purpose.

Leading versus Managing

It's important that purpose seeks a balance between risk and reward. By definition, achieving a big dream (reward) will involve a certain amount of risk and hardwork. So, the responsibility of the leader is to ensure that the resources are available to effectively manage that risk. Therefore, you need to know how to move effectively between leadership and management roles.

Much has been written about the differences between being a leader and being a manager, so we won't attempt to plow soil which has already been turned. However, we do want to emphasize that effective leaders also need to be great managers. You will not always lead – there will be times when you will need to manage.

Good management is about positively influencing processes, systems, and resources; good leadership is about positively influencing the people that drive those processes and systems – it is about the human element. Those in positions of power need to understand how to synchronize both functions.

Sean T. Hannah
Colonel, U.S. Army (Retired)
Thayer Leader Development Group at West Point

Leadership

The following guideposts are intended to illuminate when you may be serving in one role versus another:

When managing, you are:	When leading, you are:
Motivating	Inspiring
Writing policies & procedures	Building trust & maintaining loyalty
Comfort-oriented	Results-oriented
Behind the desk	In front of the troops
Protecting borders	Pushing boundaries
Answering tough questions	Asking tough questions
Pushing	Pulling
Externally directed to be compliant	Internally directed by a sense of purpose
Self-focused	Focused on others
Closed to new ideas	Open to external stimuli
Afraid to fail	Learning from past mistakes

When managing, you are:	When leading, you are:
Maintaining the status quo	Disrupting the status quo
Profit-driven	People-driven
Suppressing feelings & feedback	Expressing feelings & encouraging feedback
Staying centered on certainty	Moving toward uncertainty
Focusing on the short-term view	Focusing on the long-term view
Feeding your ego	Feeding your soul
Contractually defending relationships	Broadening & deepening relationships
Starting with "What" & "How"	Starting with "Why" (source: Simon Sinek)
Eating first	Eating last (source: Simon Sinek)
Working	Enjoying life (source: Ken Wattman)

Leadership

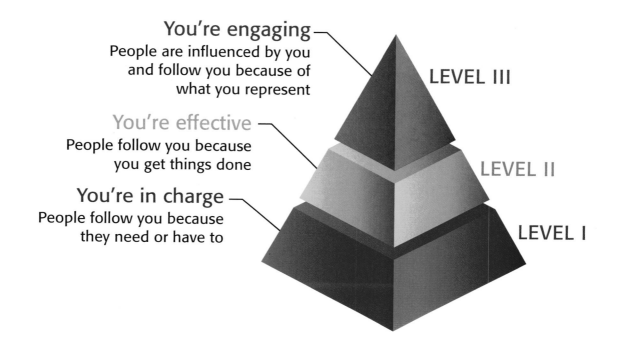

You're engaging
People are influenced by you and follow you because of what you represent

LEVEL III

You're effective
People follow you because you get things done

LEVEL II

You're in charge
People follow you because they need or have to

LEVEL I

You also need to recognize the leadership level at which you are serving. It is not uncommon to transition from one level to the next as you gain more confidence and experience in your role and you become more familiar with the people with whom you are leading. We have identified three unique levels which we refer to as Level III Leadership.

In turn, there will be times when your followers will become your source of inspiration, and will engage you. Just as your followers will feed off your leadership, so too you will feed off the leadership of your followers. When leadership flows in both directions – between leader and follower, and follower and leader – you have reached the pinnacle of successful leadership. You'll see examples of this in many of the "Applied LeaderMetrics" stories in this book.

> *If your actions inspire others to dream more, learn more, do more, and become more; you are a leader.*
> *John Quincy Adams*

> *Inspirational leadership is a serving relationship with clients that inspires their growth and makes their world a better place.*
> *Lance Secretan*

> *Good leaders make people feel that they're at the very heart of things; not at the periphery. Everyone feels that he or she makes a difference to the success of the organization. When that happens, people feel centered and that gives their work meaning.*
> *Warren Bennis*

Leadership

Born or Made?

Are leaders born or made? Researchers have concluded that the answer is, "yes" – leaders are both born and made. Leaders are likely to possess a common gene and have similar brain wave patterns. However, what nearly all leaders have in common is that they will have improved their skills over an extended period of time.

Researchers at the University College of London have isolated the gene rs4950 in a number of people who are currently serving in leadership positions. Researchers at Wake Forest have been studying the EEG scans of officers at West Point and have discovered that leaders are "wired" differently; their brain waves show that they are more decisive and better at prioritizing tasks.

However, what leaders share most in common is that they are comfortable being in a leadership role. Having a biological predisposition to serving as a leader may be a contributing factor to their success, but it's not the most important factor – it still takes hard work and practice.

We believe the importance of putting in your time is best expressed in the book, *Outliers*, by Malcom Gladwell. Malcom drew upon research conducted by Dr. K. Anders Ericsson that found a person needs to devote more than 10,000 hours of practice before they can excel at anything – be it sports, music, or business. Great leaders usually have a long history of having served in a variety of leadership roles. They didn't become "great" overnight.

Building Trust

Finally, we can't finish a section on leadership without talking about trust. Leadership and trust are inextricably linked: trust is the very essence of great leadership. You can't inspire or engage others if people don't trust you. To paraphrase Stephen M.R. Covey, the author of the bestseller *The Speed of Trust,* trust is so rare in the business world today that it has become its own currency.

Only 9%
of people believe that CEOs of major corporations are honest and can be trusted.

In a study conducted in 2013 by the Public Affairs Council, only 9% of the respondents indicated that they felt CEOs of major corporations were honest and could be trusted. (CEOs fared only modestly better than elected officials, who came in at 7%.) Yet, the same respondents said major corporations did a good job of serving their customers 65% of the time, and shareholders 63%.

Why the disconnect?

The answer is that CEOs are being perceived only as effective decision-makers – they are effective at governance, but not in a leadership or stewardship role. To build trust, followers must see that leadership, stewardship and governance are a continuum and in balance.

Leadership

One of Don's favorite formulas for explaining how you can become a trusted leader comes from a 2012 blog post by Kevin Chapman: *The 3 Ls of Leadership: Love, Listen and Leap* (forbes.com).

The first time he saw the post it reminded him of the famous Budweiser commercial that first aired in 1995 in which "Johnny" tried to talk his father and brother out of their last beer: "I love you man."

Johnny: Dad.
Dad: Yep.

Johnny: There's something I want to tell you.
Dad: What is it, son?

Johnny: Well, Dad. You're my Dad and I love you, man.
Dad: You're not getting my *Bud Light*, Johnny.

Johnny: Frank...
Frank: Forget it, Johnny.

Kevin Chapman's blog post stuck with Don for a long time because, like some men, it takes a crowbar to pry the words "I love you" out of his mouth. Yet, he kept coming across more and more research which emphasized that love is the quintessential ingredient to genuine leadership and trust.

People can sense whether you love what you do – they can sense whether you are passionate about being of service to others – they can sense whether you love them. Without love, it is difficult to build trust.

U.S. COAST GUARD 721

721

Man Overboard

Rear Admiral Steve Branham was the Commanding Officer of the USCG Cutter Gallatin from July 1999 to July 2001. His most challenging day was when one of his crew members fell overboard and was lost at sea.

Man Overboard

We asked Rear Admiral Steve Branham, USCG (Retired) to recount a leadership event which was one of the defining moments of his career.

He told us the story of when he was the Commanding Officer of the USCG Cutter Gallatin – a 378' vessel with a crew of 15 officers and 150 enlisted men and women. They were conducting a patrol 200 miles south of Cuba with the primary objective of intercepting illegal drugs which were being clandestinely shipped from South America to the United States.

About 0600 [6:00 am] my Senior Chief Quartermaster called me. He was standing the watch on the bridge as the Officer of the Deck (OOD) [person responsible to me for the safe navigation of the cutter]. His watch started at 0400 [4:00 am]. A very competent guy.

The Senior Chief said:

> *"Captain, I cannot find our Bosun's Mate of the Watch (BMOW). He has not reported in to me in over an hour."**

I told him to immediately turn the ship around and retrace our old track [the route which had been taken during the previous two hours] and to notify the Executive Officer and to wake the crew to take muster [an accounting of all crewmembers] to determine if he was on the ship or whether anyone knew of his whereabouts. When the BMOW did not respond to the muster, we searched the ship.

He was nowhere to be found.

*BMOW is roving watch stander, the "go to person" on the deck.

Man Overboard

We then tried to reconstruct what had happened. He had come on watch at 0345 (3:45 am). We interviewed the bridge team and tried to find out when he last spoke with anyone else, and when and where he may have disappeared. We determined that he probably went missing between 0500 and 0530 (5:00 – 5:30 am). So, we developed our search area based on that information. It gave us a certain area of the ocean where we thought he might be if he had fallen overboard.

We commenced the search and launched the helicopter deployed to our ship. It had been very calm in the morning, but whitecaps were now beginning to form, which made it much more difficult to find a person floating in the water.

We searched and searched but could not find him. At 1230 (12:30 pm) we held our regularly scheduled muster. It was the most difficult muster I've had in my whole career. There was a lot of emotion. I basically told the crew:

"We are going to find him one way or another.

We are going to find him.

We are not going to leave one of ours out here."

I went from the muster to the Bridge for a few minutes and then to the Combat Information Center to talk to my boss at Atlantic Area Headquarters in Portsmouth, Virginia. I told him: "I've got to call this guy's wife and tell her he is missing."

They had been married two months.

I started to pick up the radio to do a phone patch to call his wife. In the meantime, we had a Coast Guard C-130 (four-engine fixed winged aircraft) come from Guantanamo Bay, Cuba to try to help us find him. About the time I was going to do the phone patch to the wife, our radar operator who was controlling the C-130 search, heard the C-130 aircraft commander say:

"We got him."

They had located him on their last sweep before they had to go back for fuel. We raced to his position, launched our small boat and picked him up. He was sunburned and shaken up by his ordeal, but otherwise okay.

Once we got him on board we began to reconstruct the events. We determined that he had fallen overboard around 0430 (4:30 am), and that he had been in the ocean for over 10 hours.

We also learned that he was being processed for a flight physical, but was having difficulty passing the eye exam. So the ship's doctor had suggested that he not wear his glasses for several days to let his eyes adjust. The morning of the incident, the BMOW came out of the mess deck on the aft (back) end of the ship, walked forward along the starboard side, tripped over something and went over the side. He hollered as he came up sputtering, but no one heard him over the engine noise.

Man Overboard

All he saw was the stern of the ship going by.

He was wearing a light working life jacket. Unfortunately, he was not wearing the life jacket he was supposed to be wearing which was designed for the BMOW and was outfitted with signaling and survival gear.

A shark had bumped him for several hours.

When I recall that difficult day, I distinctly remember how worried and upset I was. A member of our crew was in peril. We were doing our best, but could not find him. We were determined, but the odds of finding him were diminishing quickly as the afternoon wore on and with evening approaching. Right after the noon muster, I stopped by the bridge to update my orders to the OOD. My Command Master Chief, the senior most enlisted person on the ship and a person I trusted and respected immensely, came to me on the bridgewing as I was gathering my thoughts to update our plan of action. He put his hand on my shoulder and said:

"Captain, we are going to find him. We just gotta have faith. We just have to do our mission ... what we do best. And we have to be determined. We are going to find him."

I'll never forget that. He gave me what I needed at the time – I needed support from someone I trusted, just as the crew was trusting and counting on me to find our shipmate.

Hometown
Pensacola, FL

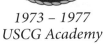

1973 – 1977
USCG Academy

1977 – 1979
USCGC GALLATIN

Steve Branham
Rear Admiral, USCG (Retired)

CASE
WESTERN
RESERVE
UNIVERSITY

*Some of the worst non-emergent
decisions I ever made were the ones
I made without seeking input from
my officers and crew. So, early on,
I learned that a collaborative and
inclusive environment produces the
best results and built that as my
personal leadership ethos that served
me well throughout my career.*

1979 – 1981
USCGC CAPE HEDGE
Commanding Officer

1984 – 1986
USCGC NEAH BAY
Commanding Officer

2008 – 2010
*Seventh Coast
Guard District
District Commander*

*2005 – 2008
Coast Guard
"CFO"*

*1999 – 2001
USCGC GALLATIN
Commanding Officer*

*1996 – 1998
USCGC HARRIET LANE
Commanding Officer*

Stewardship is your Passion. It is your discipline and commitment to judge wisely and objectively in order to protect the long-term interests of others.

If stewardship is missing, your followers will disengage.

Stewardship

As a global society, we are in a transition where post–World War II leadership theories, models, methods and strategies no longer seem to inspire us. The profile of preferred candidates has changed to where we put more value on diverse, potentially non-traditional experiences than we may have in the past.

We believe we are at the front edge of a new movement where leaders must demonstrate that they possess the attributes we would normally associate with stewardship. For this reason, we believe it is essential to integrate stewardship with leadership.

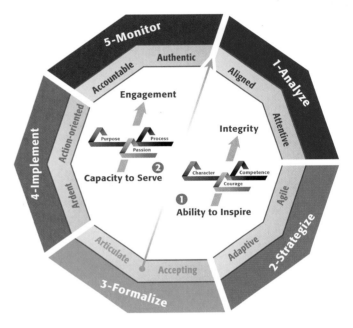

> *There is a pride in leadership; it evokes images of direction. There is humility in stewardship; it evokes images of service.*
>
> John Taft, Stewardship

Stewardship

Passion and Principles

We define stewardship as **the passion and discipline to judge wisely and objectively in order to protect and promote the long-term well-being of others.** It implies a covenant to do the right thing, with the right people, at the right time. Stewardship is the backbone to the LeaderMetrics® framework. It is what supports and makes leadership and governance genuine.

Passion is the very essence of stewardship – you cannot fake it. You either have it, or you don't. When you love your work, and the people you are working with, it will show through your actions. It will be your passion which inspires and engages others to want to follow you.

The time of the alpha male – of the dominant, typically male leader who knows everything, who gives direction to everybody and sets the pace, whom everybody follows because this person is so smart and intelligent and clever – this time is over. We need a new kind of leader who focuses much more on relationships and understands that leadership is not about himself.

Georg Vielmetter, **Leadership 2030**

Passion is fueled by your core principles – the gut-level, heartfelt values which serve as the foundation for how you conduct your life. Like ethos, you are going to be known for your principles, and your true identity will eventually be revealed. What great stewards share in common with leaders is that they are deliberate in the articulation and communication of their principles, and understand the full extent of their influential power. This suggests that genuine stewardship is dependent upon a leader living his or her principles so that they can readily act in accordance with those values.

> *You can only become truly accomplished at something you love. Don't make money your goal. Instead, pursue the things you love doing, and then do them so well that people can't take their eyes off you.*
>
> *Maya Angelou*

> *Only an organization with a sterling reputation of trust can engender a culture of client loyalty. Trust gets to the core roots of ethical behavior and integrity.*
>
> *Stephen M.R. Covey, **Speed of Trust***

Stewardship

Understand that your hard-core principles will come at a cost. Honesty and integrity will often result in short-term losses because of the additional expenditure of time, people and money to do a job right. It may also result in your losing your job if you are asked to turn a blind eye to an ethical breach. In either case, your hard-core principles will define who you are and will be essential to your long-term success.

You need to be able to identify and clearly communicate your hard-core principles so that your followers understand how they can contribute, and what will be considered acceptable behavior. This is known as *setting the tone at the top*. In order for a principles-based culture to succeed, leaders have to lead by example. Conversely, the root cause for failed organizations often is the unethical behavior of its managers.

You may recall that in the fall of 2012, a number of high ranking military officers were found to have been involved in unethical breaches. Then Secretary of Defense Leon Panetta ordered a review of existing ethics training programs, and sent a memo to the Chairman of the Joint Chiefs of Staff: *I seek your views on how to better foster a culture of value-based decision-making and stewardship among senior general and flag officers and their staffs.*

Secretary Panetta's choice of words is very interesting. You would think that he would have chosen words like, "We have a crisis in leadership" or "We have an ethics crisis" – but, instead he used the words "**value-based decision-making and stewardship**". He recognized that our military leaders are entrusted stewards of immense power and responsibility.

Other Points of Inspiration

⚌ Passion is contagious – so is complacency.
  - Mark Miller, greatleaderserve.org

⚌ Customers and employees are both demanding a greater sensitivity to their unique needs and requirements. This requires a greater alignment between leadership and stewardship.

Among the Indians there have been no written laws. Customs handed down from generation to generation have been the only laws to guide them. Anyone might act different from what was considered right if he chose to do so, but such acts would bring upon him the censure of the Nation. This fear of the Nation's censure acted as a mighty band, binding all in one social, honorable compact.

George Copway, Ojibwa Chief

Stewardship

10 Stewardship Attributes

We define an attribute as a quality or characteristic which can be observed. A great deal of leadership literature is devoted to the qualities of a leader; qualities which are not easily displayed. However, it is through both words and observable actions that we inspire others to follow.

We have conducted our own research on the stewardship attributes which we believe are essential for aligning leadership with governance. We began our research in 2012 when John Taft released his book, ***Stewardship***. We realized that his approach to the subject introduced a new dimension. Rather than developing a two-dimensional model (leadership and governance) we saw the significance and advantage of developing a three-dimensional framework – what we now refer to as LeaderMetrics®.

In 2012, we started a news aggregation portal (3ethos.com) to capture what we believe were the best stories, blogs and videos on the subjects of leadership and decision-making. What we soon discovered were the number of stories which were listing leadership attributes that didn't align with the traditional concept of a leader – they were more aligned with John Taft's concept of stewardship. With that discovery, we began to research the attributes which best define the essence of stewardship.

There were a number of questions which came to mind as we started our work:

Could we identify attributes which would be applicable to any domain – corporations, not-for-profits, government agencies and the military?

Would it be possible to identify attributes which are applicable to both effective leaders and decision-makers? Or, would we need to produce two separate lists?

Could our list of attributes reflect the direction society is moving with regards to what it prefers to see in its leaders?

In developing our list, we started by identifying all the words which are used in psychometric instruments to assess the strengths and weaknesses of leaders. For example, an instrument might measure 23 different behaviors of a leader – we would then add those behaviors to our list, removing any words which appeared on another list. In total, we found more than 200 discrete words which are used to define the characteristics and behaviors of a leader.

We then made a separate list of the attributes of highly effective decision-makers, and compared the two lists. What we looked for were the words which appeared on both lists.

We ended up identifying **10 attributes**:

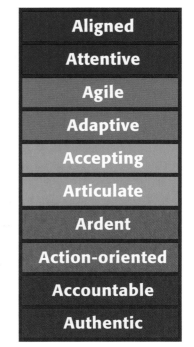

Aligned
Attentive
Agile
Adaptive
Accepting
Articulate
Ardent
Action-oriented
Accountable
Authentic

10 Stewardship Attributes

Stewardship

1. Aligned

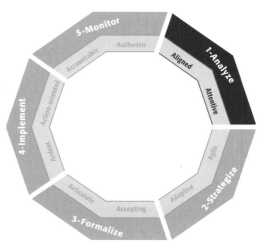

- ⚑ Has humility, situational awareness and sense of mission

- ⚑ Understands the role of other key decision-makers

- ⚑ Has a respect for objectives, standards, and policies

Great leaders and stewards understand that a mission needs to be aligned with a defined purpose and be consistent with stated principles and values. Goals and objectives have to be aligned with the interests of customers, employees and other stakeholders – not just shareholders. And, defined goals and objectives need to reflect current opportunities, challenges, rules, regulations and market conditions.

For the enterprise to achieve its fullest expression, good stewardship, high professional standards, and trust must suffuse an entire organization, from the mailroom to the boardroom. The qualities must be built into the character of the enterprise, not grafted onto its exterior.

John Bogle

2. Attentive

- ⚛ Collects and organizes data quickly and intuitively

- ⚛ Anticipates, analyzes and prioritizes conflicting priorities

- ⚛ Plans alternative contingencies

Great leaders and stewards notice everything, genuinely want to connect deeply with people, and give their undivided attention in an effort to understand others. Our friend, Bob Seaberg, refers to this as the Relational Arts; a leader must be a great listener, observer and empathizer. To be able to empathize is a fundamental emotional intelligence skill. There is no understanding and comprehension without empathy. It is the capacity to see and understand the experience, ideas and values of others.

I've learned that people will forget what you said; people will forget what you did; but, people will never forget how you made them feel.

Maya Angelou

Stewardship

3. Agile

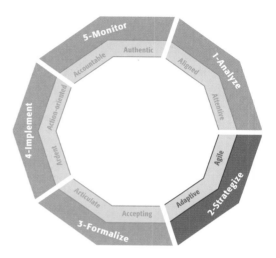

- ⚎ Takes a balanced approach to decision-making

- ⚎ Is a conceptual thinker and a theoretical problem solver

- ⚎ Sponsors collaboration

Great leaders and stewards have the capacity to balance risk with reward. They demonstrate tremendous resilience when plans go awry, oftentimes coming back stronger than before.

True genius resides in the capacity for evaluation of uncertain, hazardous, and conflicting information.
Winston Churchill

4. Adaptive

⚠ Is deliberative, practical and proactive

⚠ Quickly absorbs new information

⚠ Deals effectively with abstract concepts

Great leaders and stewards are comfortable engaging others with diverse opinions and views. Leaders are smart, but they don't feel a need to demonstrate that they are the smartest person in the room.

Leadership should be born out of the understanding of the needs of those who would be affected by it.

Marian Anderson

Stewardship

5. Accepting

⚠ Bears uncertainty with fortitude and calm

⚠ Resists the temptation to interject a personal agenda

⚠ Values diversity and the inclusion of different worldviews

Great leaders and stewards are not afraid to fail, and use setbacks as learning experiences. They have coping skills, a high tolerance for risk, and are not afraid to pivot as new ideas and challenges are presented.

Vulnerability is the birthplace of innovation, creativity and shame.

Brene Brown, Ph.D.

6. Articulate

⚠ Is persuasive in the spoken and written word

⚠ Customizes communication to the audience

⚠ Is affable, cordial, and has a sense of humor

Great leaders and stewards have the ability to share their vision and sense of purpose, and do so with an economy of words.

King: *I have a dream.*

Reagan: *Tear down this wall!*

Valvano: *Don't give up. Don't ever give up.*

Communication is the real work of leadership.
Nitin Nohria

Stewardship

7. Ardent

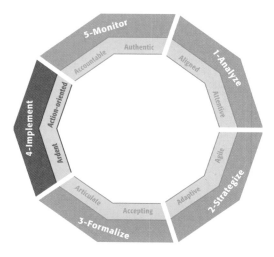

- ⬨ Is earnest, consistent, reliable, energetic and stays on track

- ⬨ Focuses on achieving goals and objectives – but does not micromanage

- ⬨ Keeps a sense of perspective in the face of adversity

Great leaders and stewards are persistent and determined. They never give up on their vision and are willing to withstand opposition from others. They press on while others quit. They also are positive thinkers, which contributes to their ability to look past the risks associated with a situation and see a more optimistic outcome.

Be daring, be different, be impractical, be anything that will assert integrity of purpose and imaginative vision against the play-it-safers, the creatures of the commonplace, the slaves of the ordinary.

Sir Cecil Beaton

8. Action-oriented

⚜ Is a self-starter

⚜ Champions new initiatives

⚜ Is assertive and results oriented

Great leaders and stewards are decisive and know how to fix problems. They are willing to move forward when others still want to gather more facts. They also focus on those things which can be controlled, and don't get hung up on missed opportunities.

What does the organization, my stakeholders, need me to be today: a coach, a teacher, a decision-maker, a supporter, a listener, a pilgrim, a servant, someone who makes waves?

Ken Melrose, On Becoming a Servant Leader

Stewardship

9. Accountable

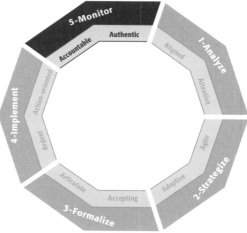

⚠ Takes and assumes responsibility

⚠ Is budget and ROI conscious

⚠ Makes optimal use of people and resources

Great leaders and stewards follow through and are responsible. They also make their followers feel safe – they make the perimeter secure.* Their words and actions are consistent. They don't ask anything from their followers that they wouldn't be willing to do themselves.

Source: Simon Sinek

Leadership should not be done purely for personal gain or goal accomplished: it should fulfill a much higher purpose.

Ken Blanchard

10. Authentic

- Is genuine, sincere, honest and free from pretense

- Has a reputation as a credible source

- Is confident

Of the ten attributes, we believe this is the most important – great leaders and stewards are genuine. What they do in public is consistent with what they do in their private life; they treat customers and clients the same way they treat staff and employees.

Leadership consists not in degrees of technique, but in traits of character; it requires moral rather than athletic or intellectual effort, and it imposes on both leader and follower alike the burdens of self-restraint.

Lewis H. Lapham

Stewardship

Yes, all the attributes start with "A". That was not one of our initial objectives; it just worked out that way.

Integrity

CHARACTER   COMPETENCE

COURAGE

Ability to Inspire   ①

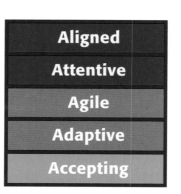

| Aligned |
| Attentive |
| Agile |
| Adaptive |
| Accepting |

Stewardship Attributes
associated with the
Ability to Inspire

We also discovered that five of the attributes effectively illuminate the leadership tenet – **The Ability to Inspire** – and, five support the engagement tenet – **The Capacity to Serve**.

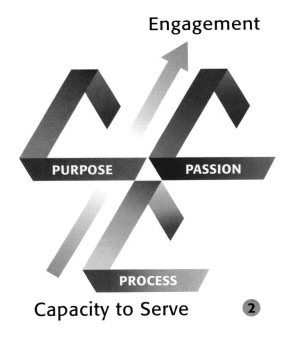

Engagement

Capacity to Serve ②

Stewardship Attributes associated with the Capacity to Serve

Stewardship

And, that each Step of the 5-Step Governance framework also was supported by two specific Stewardship Attributes.

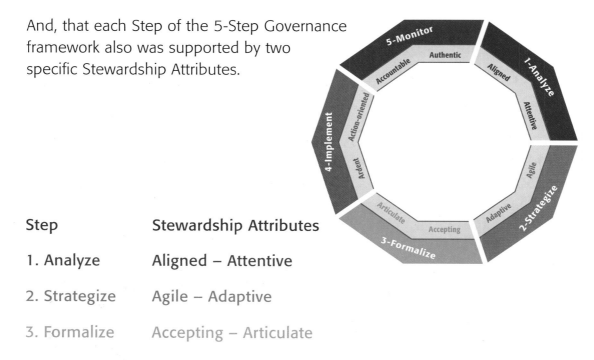

Step	Stewardship Attributes
1. Analyze	**Aligned – Attentive**
2. Strategize	Agile – Adaptive
3. Formalize	Accepting – Articulate
4. Implement	Ardent – Action-oriented
5. Monitor	**Accountable – Authentic**

Maintaining Loyalty

We finished the last section by talking about what it takes to build trust. We're going to finish this section by discussing what it takes to maintain loyal clients, employees, stakeholders and shareholders.

The prerequisite is trust. If your clients or employees don't trust you, there is no way they are going to be loyal. Simple, yet the vast majority of companies fail to understand this principle. They feel that they can gloss over breaches of trust with slick advertising and marketing, or feign remorse by instituting a fresh round of senior-level firings and restructuring.

Loyalty has a material impact on the bottom line. Research conducted by the Greene Consulting Group (greeneconsults.com) shows that loyal clients will:

- Stay with you longer;

- Add to their accounts;

- Take the time to become informed about your services;

- Make referrals;

You don't want a satisfied client – you want a loyal client.

Horst Schulze, founding President of Ritz Carlton – from an interview conducted by Greene Consulting Group

- Are more willing to try your new products and services;

- Forgive an occasional mistake;

- Tend to be insensitive to price differentials; and

- Tend to be insensitive to the pitches of your competitors.

So, besides trust, what else does it take to maintain the loyalty of your team and clients? How do you build a corporate culture which thrives on loyalty? The answer is to exhibit the ten attributes – the same ten attributes which are associated with Stewardship. Once you have built trust, you maintain loyalty by continuing to be:

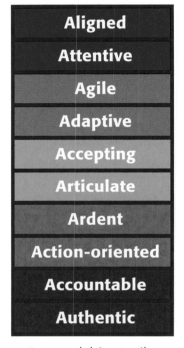

Aligned
Attentive
Agile
Adaptive
Accepting
Articulate
Ardent
Action-oriented
Accountable
Authentic

10 Stewardship Attributes

Good leaders have always stepped out of their comfort zones, but converging global megatrends are putting more pressure on those at the top to navigate a faster, more complex, more integrated, and more transparent business world.

Georg Vielmetter, Leadership 2030

Applied LeaderMetrics®

Where Everything Matters

In normal day-to-day life,
very rarely it seems are
we in situations where
everything matters.

Where Everything Matters

In April 2014, Jim Lumberg, a successful, soft-spoken businessman from Chicago, went to Nepal to join eleven other Westerners to climb Mt Everest. The group was supported by twenty-two Sherpa, three professional guides, and a base camp staff, which brought the expedition team to more than forty people. We interviewed Jim shortly after his return:

The draw to climb the mountain was very clear to me.

In normal day-to-day life, very rarely it seems are we in situations where everything matters.

When climbing a big mountain like Mt. Everest, everything matters. Relationships matter. Trust in others and being trustworthy matters. Success demands high levels of competence, a disciplined approach and process, and a deep passion for when the going gets tough. Big mountains are a place where the tenets of leadership and stewardship are not theoretical but lived and experienced. I witnessed these principles firsthand through our guides and Sherpa on Mt. Everest in the crucible of events that marked the deadliest season ever in the history of the mountain.

I learned a lot about the importance of relationships while on Mt. Everest. I reported to Kathmandu, Nepal, two weeks before I was to begin climbing the mountain. Our guides established immediately that we were expected to think of ourselves not as individual climbers but rather as a member of a team. They kept talking about stewardship and the importance of caring for our fellow climbers.

Where Everything Matters

We each had responsibilities not just for our own well-being, but for the safety and security of each other. We were reminded that an individual can accomplish a lot more as a member of a team, and there is a level of safety that comes from being in trusted relationships with others. We were required to demonstrate stewardship and care for each other: our fellow climbers, the guides, and, too, our Sherpa team members. Little did I know at the time that I would soon witness and live these principles in very real and unexpected ways.

Trust, common purpose and working together are rooted in relationships that one has to build. It just does not happen on its own. So we set off for a two week trek to Everest Base Camp to develop relationships and to learn the processes and disciplines that would be required of us once we were on the mountain. At first it was really simple stuff, like the importance of showing up on time. Most of us don't think about punctuality much, but on a big mountain, if you show up a few minutes late that means your teammates have been waiting for you, and at high altitudes that means people are getting cold and that leads to bad outcomes. Process, mutual responsibility, and relationships were the foundation we established before ever getting to the mountain. It would be really important to our chances for success, and survival.

We asked a lot of the Sherpa and our guides. We asked that they climb on the mountain and take more risk than we were going to take. We asked them to take us to the top and return us safely on a very dangerous mountain.

It was a big "ask."

What was being instilled in us over the two week trek to Everest Base Camp was an understanding of the responsibility and stewardship associated with the "ask." It was not a one-way street.

In the spirit of building relationships, Western climbers are invited to participate in the Sherpa Puja ceremony – a ritual performed before climbing an 8,000 meter (26,240 feet) mountain, where the Sherpa ask the mountain goddess for safe passage and permission to climb.

The Sherpa Puja ceremony

The ceremony includes the building of an altar, the burning of incense, and ritual chants and prayers. I didn't understand the prayers or chants, but I did understand the depth of the Sherpa's spirituality and reverence.

Where Everything Matters

And we were invited to participate with the Sherpa as teammates. The ceremony was an important event and it marked the official start of our climbing expedition. The next day the Sherpa would begin climbing through the Khumbu Icefall in advance of the Western climbers to establish our first camps on the mountain.

It would turn out to be the deadliest day in the history of Mt. Everest.

The Khumbu Icefall is the most dangerous part of the mountain, by far. It is the first section encountered on the South Col Route, the same route that was pioneered by Tenzing Norgay and Edmund Hillary. There are three cardinal rules for climbing in the Khumbu Icefall:

Always stay clipped into the rope – no matter what – because if you fall, it is your only safety line.

Keep moving – do not congregate or stop – so as to minimize the amount of time in the Icefall and being subjected to danger.

Spread out – so that if something happens, it will not take out a big group of people, and the remaining people can organize a rescue.

This is a picture of our Sherpa team following our Puja ceremony and one day before the Icefall accident. Twelve hours after this picture was taken five of these Sherpa were killed in the Icefall.

Where Everything Matters

During their climb through the Icefall, the Sherpa came to one of the ladder crossings near the top of the section and determined that the ladder placement was too dangerous for the Western climbers who would be following soon thereafter. In an act of ultimate stewardship and care for others, the Sherpa decided to rework the crossing, so they stopped and unclipped from the ropes to perform the work that needed to be done to make the passage safer for others.

The Khumbu Icefall

They broke all three rules so that Western climbers, like me, could pass more safely. At this point a massive block of ice from the Icefall collapsed, killing sixteen Sherpa – five from our team. It was the deadliest single accident ever on Mt. Everest.

You hear about Sherpa saving Western climbers. But what I witnessed next was a different situation, the guides responded to calls for help and exposed themselves to extreme danger in an effort to rescue the Sherpa. There was no hesitation. It was an equally powerful exhibition of stewardship and care for others.

Just as the Sherpa had taken risks on our behalf, the guides in trying to rescue the Sherpa unclipped, stopped, and congregated in a very dangerous place. They took incredible risks. To me, it demonstrated in a very impactful way the reciprocity of trusted relationships and the responsibility of caring and serving others. It also brought home the importance of having a process in place in advance of things going wrong. Immediately after the Icefall collapse our guides launched into a well-rehearsed rescue operation. We watched our guides throughout the morning risk everything to respond to the Sherpa. Then we watched soberly all afternoon as a helicopter removed bodies—one by one—from the Icefall. The bodies dangled lifelessly at the end of a long rope as they passed overhead.

There was deep sadness.

There was heartbreak in a way that I have not seen before. The Sherpa community is small and tightknit. Each expedition typically assembles a team from a single village so there were brothers, fathers and sons working together. Our two cooks were killed. There was a son who discovered the body of his father by identifying his boots protruding from the ice.

The Sherpa were simply heartbroken.

After responding to the Sherpa, our guides focused their attention on the climbers to help us in unexpected ways. They helped us process the day's events and make good decisions on how to respond.

Where Everything Matters

It is difficult to explain, but anyone who tries to climb an 8,000-meter peak, a big mountain, must have the mental discipline to keep pushing forward in the face of difficulty. You have to have the mindset that no matter what happens, no matter what comes your way, you are going to keep climbing. There will be times when you want to quit, but you can't.

For some of us our initial reaction was that we had to keep climbing, if for no other reason than to honor the Sherpa. But on the other hand, how can you proceed in the wake of such a tragic event? It was an emotional and confusing time.

The guides led us through a decision process that enabled us to process the events and ultimately make the right decision.

When we processed the significance of what had happened, we decided as a team not to climb. For me, that was an interesting decision-making process. We had to work through that and I was grateful for the guidance.

I was struck by the role of our guides in helping us make the right decision.

Sometimes you need a guide to help you through the thought process of making the right decision. Our guides knew immediately that our expedition was over. There was no question in their minds. However, they gave us two or three days to reach our own conclusion and guided us through the decision-making process that got us to the right place.

Jim receiving a traditional blessing from Lama Geshi. This is an important ceremony for climbers and Sherpa. Lama Geshi has blessed thousands of climbers over decades. Notice pictures in the background, many of whom are climbing legends.

When we made the decision that our expedition was over, we had a choice: we could fly out the next morning on a helicopter, or we could walk out and retrace the long trek back down the valley. The decision for me was easy—I needed time to process the experience. I just was not ready to leave. There were wounds that needed to heal. I wanted time to reflect on what had happened and to process and understand lessons from the experiences. I wanted time to be in the valley and to be in the culture.

During the week that it took to walk out of the Khumbu Valley and many times since, I have reflected on the lessons from Mt. Everest. I learned a lot about the essence of stewardship and the how effective leaders inspire and serve others. I witnessed the highest standards of character, competence and courage in action. I better understand the power and possibilities of when passion is aligned with a strong purpose and a well-established process.

Where Everything Matters

I also understand better now that you don't have to go to Mt. Everest—or any other distant place—to put these lessons to work. We have opportunities to serve and lead and inspire in ways that matter in our everyday lives.

Authors' Postscript:

We have a mutual friend, Jo Forrest, who is a pastor at Kenilworth Union Church outside of Chicago. She has interviewed CEOs of not-for-profit, for-profit, professional services, healthcare, and advertising companies to start a forum to strengthen the role of faith within one's professional life called *Chicago Faith and Leadership*.

Several themes consistent with Jo's research of CEOs resonate with Jim's story. First, faith is important in managing their work–life balance, and a source of courage when handling difficult ethical situations.

Faith is a vital part of how these CEO's show up everyday.

And second, the importance of finding ways to replenish one's faith – whether it's climbing a mountain or setting aside a day each week for meditation and relaxation. The Buddhists have a saying:

You cannot pour from an empty cup.

Nurturing one's faith provides the opportunity to say "yes" to new things, and to help heal emotional wounds.

James Lumberg
Co-Founder
Executive Vice President

ENVESTNET

*Hometown
Edgewater, CO*

SMU.
*1984 – 1987
B.A.
Southern Methodist University*

*1987 – 1989
M.A.
Harvard University*

"In normal day-to-day life, very rarely are we in situations where everything matters."

*1989 – 1991
(prior to the War)
Missionary in Liberia, Africa*

NUVEEN
Investments
*1991 – 2000
Director, Fixed Income
Mutual Funds*

*2014
Everest Climb*

*2001 – Present
Co-Founder of the
Kilimanjaro English School
in Moshi, Tanzania*

Governance is your prudent decision-making Process.

If missing, followers will feel confused.

Governance

One of the important values of our LeaderMetrics® framework is its utility – the decision-making process can be used in any important endeavor, no matter the industry sector or domain. When properly implemented, it will significantly increase the odds of developing a strategy which can withstand the test of private and public scrutiny.

In this section we are going to provide clear guidance to a governance framework consisting of 5 Steps and 17 Dimensions (Dimensions are the details to a step).

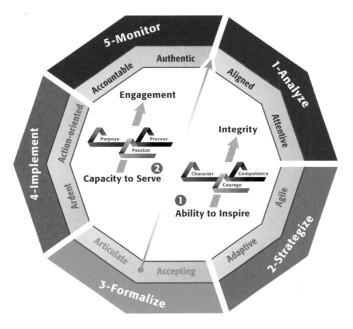

Governance

Your leadership and stewardship role is to maximize the benefit to be gained from the governance framework – that is, to maximize the likelihood of achieving defined goals and objectives. It will be your actions as the leader and steward of the decision-making process which will have the greatest impact on success.

Governance is often associated with rules, regulations and principles, so it's important to define the differences between the terms:

Rules are used to constrict behavior, and require the least amount of discernment – they do not require that a person be able to judge wisely and objectively.

Regulations are used to control behavior, and require that a person have some ability to discern right from wrong.

Principles are used to guide behavior and require that a person have a moral compass.

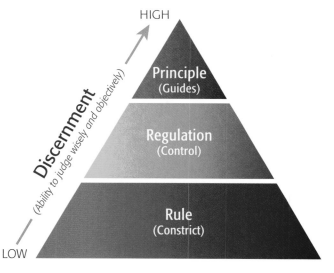

The choice as to whether a governance framework is defined by rules, regulations or principles is critically important because it will have an impact on morale and behavior. Rules can communicate to followers that you don't trust their judgment and, as a result, they will likely act inappropriately.

Our human nature drives us to test rules. When given a rule, a lot people begin to think of exceptions. Principles, on the other hand, imply to followers that you trust their judgment, which, in turn, tends to produce better behavior. To illustrate the important differences between rules and principles, consider the following two statements:

Thou shall not kill

Love one another

Which is a rule, and which is a principle? Where does your mind go when you read the rule, *Thou shall not kill*? You probably start thinking of exceptions: What about in a time of war? What about in self-defense? What about as a form of punishment for a person who has murdered another? On the other hand, where does your mind go when you hear the principle, *Love one another*. It's more difficult to think of an exception.

Governance

When mores [customs and cultures of a society] are sufficient, laws are unnecessary; when mores are insufficient, laws are unenforceable.

Emile Durkheim

Too many rules get in the way of leadership. They just put you in a box. ... People set rules to keep from making decisions.

"Coach K" (Duke Basketball Coach Mike Krzyzewski)

Society depends upon professionals to provide reliable fixed standards in situations where the facts are murky or the temptations too strong. Their principal contribution is an ability to bring sound judgment to bear on these situations. They represent the best a particular community is able to muster in response to new challenges.

Dr. Robert Kennedy, St. Thomas University

7 hints you're about to make the wrong decision as a leader:

1. It makes everyone happy.

2. It's easy.

3. You made it alone.

4. You made it too quickly.

5. You made it too slowly.

6. It changed nothing.

7. Your gut tells you otherwise.

Source: Ron Edmondson (ronedmondson.com)

Governance

When there is a low trust environment, the result is often more rules and regulations and the creation of a compliance and checklist mentality. *If I can put a check in the box, I'm safe. I must be "okay."* Paraphrasing Stephen M. R. Covey, *compliance becomes the prosthesis for a lack of trust.* Under such conditions, there is a tension which inhibits the emergence of authentic leadership.

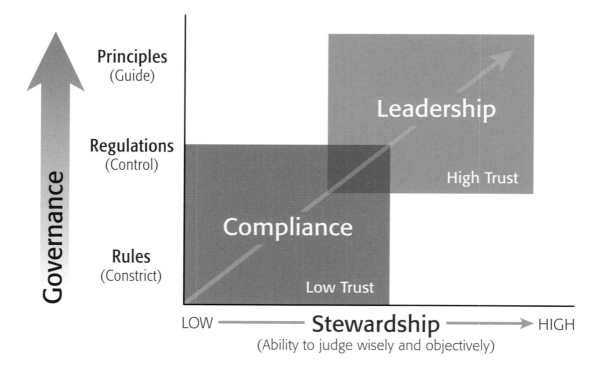

The same is true for the differences between a code of ethics and a code of conduct. A code of conduct is normally written for a low trust environment and is based on rules. A code of ethics is based on principles. Often organizations state that they have a code of ethics, but upon reading, it is obvious that they have written a code of conduct.

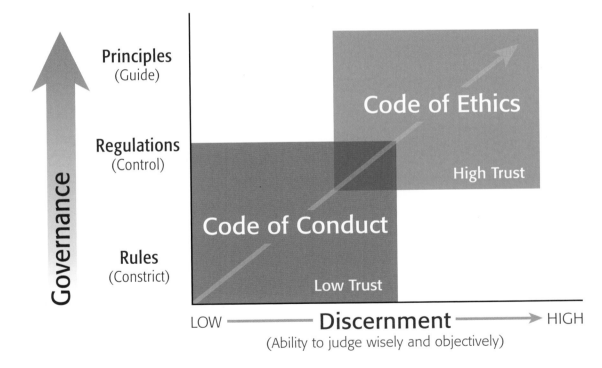

Other Points of Inspiration

- Lesson from Katrina: With regards to governance, "simple" is preferable to "complex" when operating in a difficult and dynamic environment.

- Good governance should bring clarity to what appears to be chaos.

- If you lack the time, inclination or the knowledge to become familiar with a strategy, delegate to an expert.

- We caution you not to fall into a "checklist mentality"— putting a checkmark in a box without fully investigating the appropriateness or completeness of a procedure.

- We believe that layers of rules and regulations, including rules-based codes of conduct, only make it easier for dishonest actors to go undiscovered.

- Superior performance is often the result of developing a prudent process or strategy, and then adhering to it. Only by following a structured process can you be certain that all critical components of a strategy are being properly implemented.

- When directors, trustees and fiduciaries have been sued for their decision-making process, it often has been because of an omission as opposed to a commission – it wasn't from what they did, but what they forgot to do. Hence the importance of a defined framework.

Governance

Five Steps – 17 Dimensions

The governance framework we are going to share with you comes from our collective experiences – the more than sixty years the two of us have served as officers, managers, executives, and directors.

In turn, it also is based on our familiarity with the legal requirements associated with a fiduciary standard of care. One of the requirements of a fiduciary standard is that decision-makers must show the details of their decision-making process. It was this requirement which prompted Don to spend the last twenty-seven years perfecting the language of a governance process which could be used to substantiate a legal standard of care. The result is our governance framework consisting of 5 Steps and 17 Dimensions.

Governance

STEP 1. ANALYZE

We start by defining what we want to accomplish in terms of goals and objectives, taking into consideration current facts and circumstances. We then identify who the key decision-makers are going to be, and ensure that they know what regulations, policies and procedures may impact their decision-making process.

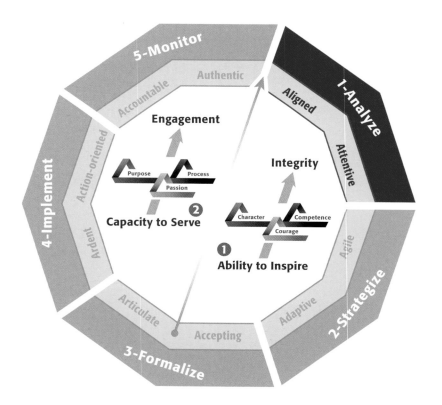

STEP 1. ANALYZE

Dimensions (Details of the Step)

1.1: State goals and objectives

1.2: Define roles and responsibilities of decision-makers

1.3: Brief decision-makers on objectives, standards, policies, and regulations

Stewardship Attributes: Aligned — Attentive

To succeed, your goals and objectives must be aligned with your ethos and sense of purpose, and then communicated to key decision-makers. You should expect that decision-makers will represent a diversity of acumen, education, background and experience so you need to be attentive and inclusive of their different world views, and respect and give careful consideration to dissenting opinions. Once everyone is aligned, it's important that you brief decision-makers on the need for the goals to be consistent with relevant policies, procedures and regulations.

Governance

STEP 2. STRATEGIZE

In this next Step, all factors should be identified which may have a bearing on the strategy that has the greatest probability of accomplishing the defined goals. There are four Dimensions to this Step; to help you remember the four inputs, we have created the acronym **RATE**:

R – Risk   **A** – Assets   **T** - Time Horizon   **E** - Expected Outcomes

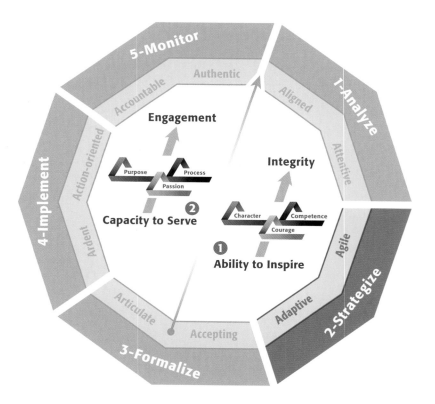

STEP 2. STRATEGIZE

Dimensions (Details of the Step)

2.1: Identify sources and levels of *Risk*

2.2: Identify *Assets*

2.3: Identify *Time Horizons*

2.4: Identify *Expected Outcomes*

Stewardship Attributes: Agile — Adaptive

In developing the best strategy to accomplish defined goals and objectives, a number of inputs need to be factored — Risks, Assets, Time Horizon and Expected Outcomes. As new inputs and information are gathered and analyzed there will very likely be a need to revise the strategy which is being considered. This requires decision-makers to be able to think outside the box and be willing to try new ideas.

Governance

STEP 3. FORMALIZE

The third Step is to develop a strategy which represents the greatest probability of achieving defined goals and objectives; is consistent with the RATE inputs (Risks, Assets, Time Horizon and Expected Outcomes); and, can be realistically implemented and monitored. Once these conditions are satisfied, the strategy needs to be clearly communicated to key decision-makers and stakeholders. Great decision-makers develop clear, unambiguous strategies.

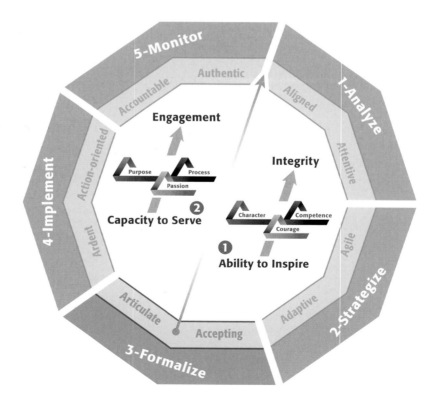

STEP 3. FORMALIZE

Dimensions (Details of the Step)

3.1: Define the strategy that is consistent with RATE

3.2: Ensure the strategy is consistent with implementation and monitoring constraints

3.3: Formalize the strategy in detail and communicate

Stewardship Attributes: Accepting — Articulate

Great leaders accept the fact that every strategy is subject to factors which are beyond the leader's ability to predict or control, and yet they have the courage to move forward. The greatest risk associated with any strategy is omission — leaving something vital out. This is one of the reasons why it is critical for key decision-makers and stakeholders to have an opportunity to provide input into the development of the strategy. Leaders must be able to simply and clearly articulate the strategy.

Governance

STEP 4. IMPLEMENT

What starts out as strategy must be translated into reality through implementation. Once formalized, the next step is to identify the experts required to implement the strategy. Key personnel will need to be provided with appropriate tools, budgets and resources to execute. This is when management skills are essential. When it becomes necessary to prepare agreements or contracts, extra care should be taken to ensure that terms are consistent with defined goals and objectives and that all parties understand their role and responsibilities.

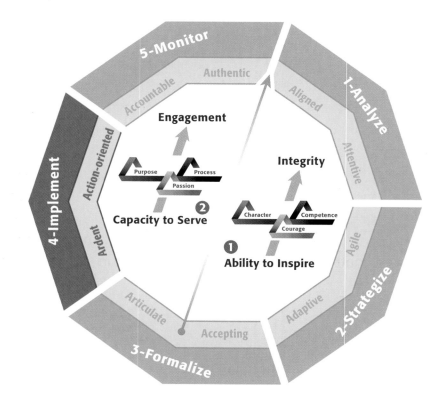

STEP 4. IMPLEMENT

Dimensions (Details of the Step)

4.1: Define the process for selecting key personnel to implement the strategy

4.2: Define the process for selecting tools, methodologies, and budgets to implement the strategy

4.3: Ensure that service agreements and contracts do not contain provisions which conflict with objectives

Stewardship Attributes: Ardent — Action-oriented

Once the defined strategy has been agreed upon and communicated, it needs to be implemented by those who are most qualified, ready, willing and able. We would strongly encourage you to follow the time-proven maxim of doing what you do best, and delegate the rest to other qualified professionals. The leader has the added responsibility to ensure that those who are implementing the strategy have the proper resources and tools to accomplish their defined goals and objectives, and that their efforts are properly supported and protected by agreements and contracts. Leaders need to be ardent in delegating and action-oriented in implementing.

Governance

STEP 5. MONITOR

Great leaders remain open to changing a strategy in the presence of new facts. You are responsible for periodically assessing the progress being made to achieve defined goals and objectives, and to ensure that the work is being performed within budget. Here transparency is critical so that all stakeholders are aware of current progress. You will also need to periodically assess whether there:

- ♨ Are conflicts of interests or ethical violations involving key decision-makers;
- ♨ Is a degradation of morale or performance;
- ♨ Is a need for intervention and action;
- ♨ Is a need to change the strategy.

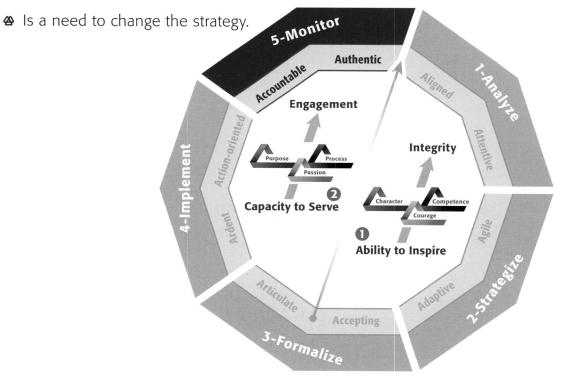

STEP 5. MONITOR

Dimensions (Details of the Step)

5.1: Prepare periodic reports that compare performance with objectives

5.2: Prepare periodic reports that analyze costs, or ROI, with performance and objectives

5.3: Conduct periodic examinations for conflicts of interest and self-dealing, and breaches of a code of ethics

5.4: Prepare periodic qualitative reviews or performance reviews of decision-makers

Stewardship Attributes: Accountable — Authentic

Key decision-makers should always be kept aware of the progress being made toward meeting defined goals and objectives – not only knowing what has happened, but why. You need to control and account for all expenses and be mindful of budgetary constraints. You also need to periodically assess whether the strategy being implemented, and the people involved, remain aligned with the organization's ethos. In the words made famous by Ronald Reagan: **Trust but verify.** [Reagan was told that Russians like to use proverbs when they communicate, so he selected the Russian proverb – *doveryai no proveryai* – trust but verify.] Leaders need to be true to their style and beliefs – authentic in monitoring themselves and others.

Governance

Our governance framework is simple, yet it can be used to develop and execute even the most complex strategies. Good governance requires that you maintain a rational consistent decision-making process.

So too, it can be used in any domain — to define an investment strategy; outline a business plan; inform directors of their role; even to help prospective commanding officers of military units prepare to take command.

Execution is not just tactics — it is a discipline and a system. It has to be built into a company's strategy, its goals, and its culture. And the leaders of the organization must be deeply engaged in it.

Larry Bosidy, **Execution**

The Plains tribes arranged their knowledge in a circular format—which is to say, there were no ultimate terms or constituents of their universe; only sets of relationships that sought to describe phenomena. The purpose of such an arrangement was to be certain that all known aspects of something would be included in the information that people possessed and considered when making decisions and reaching conclusions.

Vine Deloria, Jr., Spirit & Reason

Governance

The Law of Decreasing Risk

The Law of Compounding Risk (developed by Robert Porter Lynch) states that complexity increases by double the number of new elements introduced in a business model. For example: The complexity of (1) launching a new product, (2) with a new partner, and (3) in a new location, increases the complexity (and therefore the likelihood of failure) by a factor of 6.

$$(N)(N-1) = \text{Compounded Risk}$$

If the *Law of Compounding Risk* is true, then the opposite – *Law of Decreasing Risk* – also should hold true: that complexity (risk) should decrease as we introduce prudent procedures to a decision-making process.

The risk of not meeting stated goals and objectives proportionally decreases by the number of governance dimensions being employed. For example, the decision-maker who (1) articulates goals and objectives, (2) clearly communicates a strategy to meet the goals and objectives, and (3) employs experts to implement the strategy can substantially reduce the risks associated with the strategy by two-thirds (2/3). The formula would be:

$$(N-1)/N = \text{Decreased Risk}$$

Risky Business

Bill knows firsthand what it
means to recover from
a life-threatening injury
on the job.

Risky Business

William (Bill) Zachry was named the 2014 Risk Manager of the Year. He received the award for the work he has done to help significantly reduce workers' compensation costs. Bill knows firsthand what it means to recover from a life-threatening injury on the job.

Bill's Dad died when he was a senior in high school, so he had to put himself through college.

One of the jobs he took was to be the playground director for Daly City, California.

On November 7, 1976, Bill arrived at 3:30 in the afternoon to open one of the city's playgrounds. Normally there would be a lot of little kids, but this particular afternoon he noticed a group of teenagers hanging out. He put on his Daly City windbreaker so he would look official and walked over. It was then that he saw two girls fighting. Bill knew that if the older kids were there, and particularly if they were fighting, the little kids would not come to the playground. So, he decided to break up the fight.

As he pulled one of the girls off of the scrum, eight guys attacked him.

Risky Business

The gang was hitting and kicking him but with very little effect. As he was backing away one of the boys kicked him pretty hard. As he turned towards that boy,

"someone turned out the sound and everything slowed down."

Bill then noticed one of his attackers was holding another back, and the guy being held had a knife in his hand with blood on it. Bill figured he had better try to escape to the clubhouse.

The gang chased him, swinging their belts with large buckles above their heads. He eventually made it to the clubhouse and locked himself in. He then called his boss and informed him that there was a problem in the park:

"Somebody got stabbed!"

It was then that he realized there was blood seeping down his side and that he was the one who had been knifed.

His boss called an ambulance and he was taken to the hospital where emergency surgery was performed to remove his spleen. Bill recounts:

"The knife had gone into the back, through the lungs, through the diaphragm and through the spleen. But, I did not know I was that severely injured at the time, because of the adrenaline."

Bill ended up spending a week in the hospital:

"That was my introduction to workers' compensation."

The California State Compensation Insurance Fund (SCIF) did the claims administration for Bill's case. Thirty years later, Bill was appointed by Governor Edmund Brown to be a board member on SCIF. He also was recently appointed as a director on the Board of Quality Assurance at the same medical facility where he had been treated.

Risky Business

Bill's first job out of college was as a workers' compensation claims adjuster. As an injured worker, and as a claims adjuster, Bill discovered:

"Most employers think that the biggest workers' compensation cost driver is due to fraud created by injured workers. Actually, the bigger fraud problems (and the largest cost drivers in the system) are caused by poor medical providers in the system. The most cost-effective workers' compensation program focuses on providing the right medical care (evidence-based medicine) at the right time to get the injured worker back to work."

In 2014, as Vice President of Risk Management for Safeway – one of the largest grocery chains in the U.S. with more than 135,000 employees – Bill received Business Insurance Magazine's *Risk Manager of the Year Award*. In his role, he began to take an interest in trying to understand why certain severely injured workers were able to return to work, while other less severely injured employees remained "disabled." Bill shared his observations with a senior medical officer for military personnel in Iraq. The officer reported that he too had observed soldiers with severe injuries and strong coping skills being able to return to duty more quickly than those who lacked coping skills and had only minor injuries.

Bill then discovered that the Centers for Disease Control and Prevention (CDC) had published an extensive study called *The Adverse Childhood Experiences Study*. The research shows that about 20% of the population has poor coping skills caused by early childhood experiences. This provided an explanation as to why certain injured workers are able to "cope" while others cannot.

Bill then set about developing an intervention process for injured workers who had been identified as having poor coping skills:

> *"Providing prompt, accurate benefits is the right thing for the injured worker. If you identify those at risk, and intervene correctly, you can significantly reduce workers' compensation costs.*
>
> *The pilot program at Safeway identified 88 at-risk individuals. Because of our intervention program, all 88 are back to work and there has been no litigation. We determined that those who go back to work, versus those who do not, has a lot to do with the individual's capacity to cope with an adverse situation. It has very little to do with the severity of the accident."*

Risky Business

The protocol to help injured workers at Safeway involves a series of questions, the answers to which help practitioners identify which workers have poor coping skills. When a worker is flagged, attending physicians are alerted so that treatment can be augmented with counseling. The net result, Safeway's workers' compensation costs are now 40% below the industry average.

Bill's parting philosophy:

> *"Do the right thing for the individual. Get them the right care; make them well; then, get them back to work so they can be successful."*

William Zachry
Vice President of
Risk Management
Safeway Inc.

*Playground
Director*

San Francisco State

*"Doing the right thing for injured
workers is actually the best way
to save money in the workers'
compensation system."*

Stanford

CALIFORNIA
**SELF-INSURERS'
SECURITY FUND**

Board of Directors

C.E. HEATH & PARTNERS
Insurance and Reinsurance Brokers

*Chair of Fraud Assessment
Commission*

**STATE
COMPENSATION
INSURANCE
FUND**

*Appointed by Governor
Jerry Brown through
January of 2019*

TheZenith℠
WORKERS' COMPENSATION SPECIALISTS

SAFEWAY®

2001 – Present

*eStellarNEt, an internet B2B
medical bill and attachment
clearinghouse for the workers'
compensation industry*

What all genuine leaders share is a strongly developed sense of self. This is particularly true during a time of stress when a person's natural behavior cannot be camouflaged.

Assessing Your Strengths and Weaknesses

An important step in developing yourself as a genuine leader, steward and decision-maker is to assess your strengths and weaknesses. You must be comfortable with who you are before you can possibly lead; who you are will have a direct impact on your ability to inspire and engage others.

What all genuine leaders share is a strongly developed sense of self. This is particularly true during a time of stress when a person's natural behavior cannot be camouflaged.

> **Leaders do not overcompensate or put on a false façade – they are Authentic and Aligned, two of our most important Stewardship Attributes.**

There are several ways you can identify and assess your strengths and weaknesses. Formal assessment tests – such as psychometric instruments, which we will discuss later – can give you insights to what comes most naturally to you, versus what you have adopted in order to fit into your environment. Discussions with mentors, peers, friends, and colleagues can enlighten you if you are open to 360° feedback and constructive insights. Also, personal reflection, journaling, as well as trial and error can help you identify when you have been most comfortable and effective in a leadership or critical decision-making role.

Assessing Your Strengths and Weaknesses

Strengths can be a gift or a curse. There may be times when you lean too heavily on your perceived strengths – referred to as *illusory superiority* – and miss opportunities, overlook ideas from people with opposing styles, or miscalculate risks. One of the best ways to deal with illusory superiority is to add members to your team who have complementary skills.

Avoiding illusory superiority is the reason why Attentive, Adaptive and Accepting are also important Stewardship Attributes.

You need to identify your weaknesses and blind spots, which also can be both a blessing and a curse. It can be a curse because when you can't see the true causes of a problem, you may underestimate risks. Any solution you try to implement may actually make matters worse. On the other hand, blind spots can be a benefit if they allow you to see a clearer vision of what might lie ahead. When others see nothing but risk, you see opportunity. You may recall the famous Apple ad – *The Crazy Ones:*

Here's to the crazy ones. The misfits. The rebels. The troublemakers. The round pegs in the square holes. The ones who see things differently. They're not fond of rules. And they have no respect for the status quo. You can quote them, disagree with them, glorify or vilify them. But the only thing you can't do is ignore them. Because they change things. They push the human race forward. And while some may see them as the crazy ones, we see genius. Because the people who are crazy enough to think they can change the world, are the ones who do.

Apple – Think Different – Richard Dreyfuss narration

Psychometric Instruments

Leadership should not be assessed in a vacuum or from afar. We believe the best way to begin is to use one or more of the 300 commercially available psychometric instruments. The results of the instrument, coupled with self-reflection and 360° feedback, are essential for you to get a clearer view of your true self.

The most widely used psychometric instruments include DISC, Kolbe, Birkman, Myers-Briggs Type Indicator (MBTI), Chally and Strength Finder. Each generally offers a convenient on-line instrument which can be completed in 20–30 minutes. These instruments have been taken by tens of thousands of participants, which is critical for validating the underlying algorithms and metrics, and for the predictive integrity of the profiles which are produced.

These instruments are not intended to measure intelligence, experience, or acumen; nor should the results be impacted by a person's education level, world views, gender or age. There is no such thing as a good or bad profile. The assessments provide you greater self-awareness, and a better understanding of how to work more effectively with others who have a different (often complementary) profile.

We typically use TTI's (ttisuccessinsights.com) DISC for our leadership development programs, including the training we conduct in affiliation with *The Thayer Leader Development Group at West Point*. For that reason, and by way of example, we're going to demonstrate how DISC can be used to assess your strengths and weaknesses.

Assessing Your Strengths and Weaknesses

DISC is an acronym for the four behaviors which are exhibited to a greater or lesser extent by every person:

Dominance – measures how you respond to problems and challenges. A person with high D tendencies will be forceful, strong-willed, direct, daring and persistent. D's are results-oriented and like to express their ideas and views projecting into the future. They like facts and figures, bullet points and brevity. They are self-starters who are innovative and competitive.

Influence – measures how you influence others. A person with high I tendencies will be persuasive, talkative, enthusiastic, sociable and emotional. I's like to work in groups and have interactive networks. When communicating with an I, socialize with them. Ask their opinion and put details in writing. I's are creative problem solvers who are optimistic and enthusiastic. They enjoy humor and are team players.

Steadiness – measures your pace and consistency. A person with high S will be predictable, systematic, serene, sincere and stable. S's like standards and methods. They prefer a stable and predictable environment and to be recognized for completed jobs and tasks. S's are best approached with logic and informality while allowing them time to think. They are good listeners, patient and dependable.

Compliance – measures how you respond to rules and procedures. A person with high C will be a perfectionist, courteous, mature, accurate, and conscientious. C's enjoy critical thinking, task-oriented work and close relationships with a small group of people. They prefer a quiet environment and tend to be technical and quality-oriented. When working with a C, you want to use data, facts and figures and provide a timetable and milestones. C's will be diplomatic and conscientious about meeting high standards for themselves and the team.

Assessing Your Strengths and Weaknesses

Given the D I S C descriptors, take a moment and think about what your DISC profile probably looks like.

Are you more of a D or a C?

Perhaps a stronger I than S?

Copied to the right are the DISC profiles of two different individuals. If you were trying to fill a sales role, which of the profiles would be the best candidate?
If you were trying to fill an accounting or office management role, which profile would be the best candidate?

It is not the critic who counts; not the man who points out how the strong man stumbles, or where the doer of deeds could have done them better. The credit belongs to the man who is actually in the arena, whose face is marred by dust and sweat and blood; who strives valiantly; who errs, who comes short again and again, because there is no effort without error and shortcoming; but who does actually strive to do the deeds; who knows great enthusiasms, the great devotions; who spends himself in a worthy cause; who at the best knows in the end the triumph of high achievement, and who at the worst, if he fails, at least fails while daring greatly, so that his place shall never be with those cold and timid souls who neither know victory nor defeat.

Theodore Roosevelt

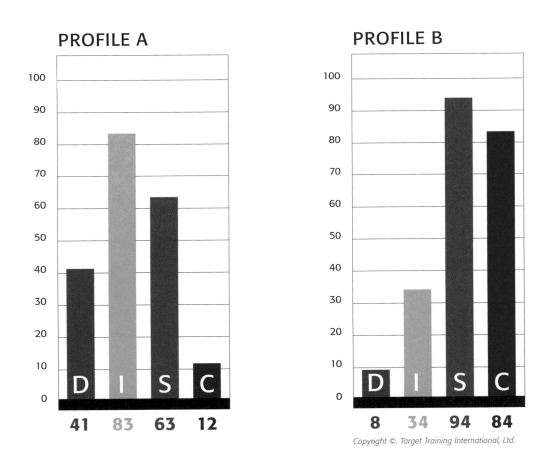

PROFILE A

D	I	S	C
41	83	63	12

PROFILE B

D	I	S	C
8	34	94	84

For the sales role, you would likely want Profile A – a candidate who is comfortable in a dominant role which requires strong people skills. For the accounting or office management position, Profile B would likely be the better candidate because of their preference to deal with details and comfort in resolving conflicts.

Assessing Your Strengths and Weaknesses

You can also use psychometric profiles to help build better teams and boards. The old adage "opposites attract" is applicable. Ideally, if you were constructing a team or board of four, you would want four people who each had a different profile. The high D may be pushing toward a goal while the high C ensures that proper procedures are being followed. The high S may bring steadiness to the group while the high I becomes a valuable resource for resolving conflicts.

When profiling is coupled with coaching and mentoring, the administration of performance reviews can be greatly improved. Without the benefit of the profiles, we are likely to rate people who are like us more highly than those who are different than us. We may miss or under-appreciate the talents and skills of people who have a different profile. For example, if a manager is a demonstrative, hard charging, big-picture person, she may diminish and discount the important work of a quiet, detail-oriented perfectionist.

The profiles can also be useful in identifying more introverted and extroverted leaders. Generally speaking, people with high D and I profiles are more likely to be extroverted than introverted, while high S and C tend to be more introverts. In the past, society has favored extrovert leaders, but we believe that is no longer the case. Many of the more effective and impactful leaders of recent history have tended to exhibit traits of an introvert – Nelson Mandela, Mother Theresa, Warren Buffet, and Bill Gates all come to mind.

There is no correlation between the best talker and those that have the best ideas.

Susan Cain, Ph.D.

Coaching

Another important step in developing yourself as a genuine leader, steward and decision-maker is to surround yourself with people who are passionate and committed to your success. Besides family, friends, colleagues and peers, you may also want to consider hiring a coach.

Coaching, as defined by the International Coach Federation (coachfederation.org), is ...*partnering with clients in a thought-provoking and creative process that inspires them to maximize their personal and professional potential.*

Coaching is different than consulting. A consultant generally has an area of expertise and provides you their answers to a particular problem. They're going to tell you what to do and how to do it. Coaching is intended to help you see future possibilities and develop in you the courage to take risks and develop a broader vision.

Research has demonstrated that

... coaching has significant positive effects on performance and skills, well-being, coping, work attitudes, and goal-directed self-regulation.

Theeboom, Beersma, and van Vianen

Assessing Your Strengths and Weaknesses

Coaching has become popular with executives and managers who find it helpful to have an independent third-party to safely bounce off bold ideas or to assist in managing difficult or stressful situations.

Coaches and coaching philosophies come in all shapes and sizes – you may want to try different people and approaches until you find a combination which works best for you. You should feel comfortable sharing weaknesses and strengths with your coach and being pushed by your coach to reach your goals.

What's important is that your coach individualizes your sessions so they are based on your goals and objectives – otherwise your "coach" may actually be a "consultant." There also is an imperative of mutual trust, confidentiality and respect between you and your coach. The two of you must also periodically assess the effectiveness of the coaching process.

Your coach will likely employ several techniques including:

Listening – Your coach will listen to extract information beyond the words you are saying to help discover passion, excitement, discomfort and insecurity. It is your coach's role to bring these emotions to the surface so they can be used to forge a more positive outcome.

Questioning – Your coach will probe with powerful questions to evoke "aha" moments. Typically the questions will be open-ended to enable you to focus on what the future may hold.

Reframing – Your coach may reframe some of your statements to demonstrate how problems can be turned into opportunities.

Your coach will hold you accountable for agreed-upon goals, actions or behavior changes. If you can incorporate coaching skills into your leadership style, you will most likely see a marked improvement in the ability of your followers to regulate and motivate themselves.

Assessing Your Strengths and Weaknesses

Choosing your Decisions – *being at choice*

An important role of a coach is to make sure you are choosing your decisions, which is sometimes called *being at choice*. For many people it is far easier to go along with others' suggestions, processes, directions or precedent.

Coaches should help you:

Develop Yourself	Influence Others
Follow your heart	Challenge the status quo
Stay true to your own values Focus and meet your goals	Have the confidence to speak up when necessary Interact with others
Establish and respect your point of view Think things through on your own	Take on challenges Being in balance with self and connect with others

When you develop yourself, you influence others by:

Inspiring with Purpose	Acting with Passion	Managing with Process
Leadership	Stewardship	Governance

Consider adopting a similar "coach approach" when you are working with clients, employees or team members. Generally people prefer to be part of a solution, not told what to do.

According to a recent study at Case Western Reserve University:

When leaders experience compassion through coaching the development of others, they experience psychophysiological effects that restore the body's natural healing and growth processes, thus enhancing their sustainability. We thus suggest that to sustain their effectiveness, leaders should emphasize coaching as a key part of their role and behavioral habits.

Smith, Boyatzis and Van Ooston
Motivating Others through Coaching with Compassion

Historically, the Six Nations Iroquois Confederacy required that chiefs consider the impact of their decisions on the seventh generation. For every decision they made, they had to consider how it would impact the families and communities that would be alive seven generations from now.

First Nations Development Institute

Master of the Sword

We are an Army of One.

Master of the Sword

Brigadier General Maureen LeBoeuf, U.S. Army (Retired), was the first woman to lead a department at the U.S. Military Academy at West Point. In 1997, she was appointed to the coveted position of *Master of the Sword* and held that position until her retirement from the Army in 2004. *Master of the Sword* is the title given to the head of the Department of Physical Education at West Point.

"The appointment had to go to Congress for approval and then it had to be signed off by the President."

When I was selected there was some pushback from old grads and there was an active email campaign to block my nomination – I was aware of that. But the Superintendent, General Dan Christman, shielded me and took a lot of heat for the decision to make me Master of the Sword. I admire him greatly because it was a bold decision. If it had been the department of English, it would have been a hiccup. But it was the department of physical education, I am a women and I am not a graduate of West Point. So, there were a couple of things that surprised people about my selection.

Master of the Sword

Needless to say, the stakes were high and many people were uncomfortable with me holding the coveted position.

When I took over as the head of the department, I would go around and watch classes. One class, in particular, caught my attention – gymnastics. There were certain lessons when the women would be on one side of the gymnasium and the men on the other. I said to the course director:

> *"You know, we don't do this in the Army – we don't separate the men and the women. We are an Army of one."*

It concerned me that during their Plebe year we were separating them. I think it sent a message and not a message I wanted the Cadets to get. So, I set up a committee to suggest what changes needed to be made to the course.

The committee met for most of the academic year. The night before the planned briefing, I was told by a confidant:

> *"You are going to get this briefing tomorrow and you're not going to like the recommendation – nothing is going to change."*

I was thankful the confidant had come forward to warn me, while at the same time I was furious at the committee. However, the advance warning gave me time to calm down. So, the next day I received the briefing and at the end I said: *"Thank you for your time."*

My retirement run. I was authorized a parade, but I asked for a run with the Corps of Cadets. The Brigade Commander is to my left and my son is to her left. Great memory!

I realized the timing wasn't right. The committee members were not ready to make any changes. Some of the civilian faculty members that taught the course had been there for three decades. I was told things like:

> *"It's the same course General Schwarzkopf took; if it was good enough for him it is good enough for our Cadets."*

And I said:

> *"That is wonderful; there were no women in the Corps then and we have a different Army and we are getting ready to enter the 21st century. We have to think differently about the way we are educating and training the Cadets."*

Master of the Sword

On the other hand, I was not going anywhere – I knew I had time. A couple of years went by and I was watching a gymnastics class with one of the instructors who was a respected civilian Ph.D. and had been a world class-gymnast in college.

He told me,

> *"If this course does not change, I cannot continue to teach it."*

At that moment, I thought: *"I've got my guy who can help me lead this change."* So, I set up a second committee.

After the first attempt to initiate change, I had conducted my own personal AAR (After Action Review). I thought about what I didn't do well in setting the whole thing up. Two things I did differently the second time is that I gave the committee a written charter of my expectations (called a Commander's Intent), and held regularly scheduled progress reviews.

The second committee came back with significant changes. They changed the name of the course from Gymnastics to Military Movement to better reflect what the course was all about. There were also certain lessons when the Cadets would wear their battle dress uniform, including boots, and carrying a weapon.

We quickly observed that the Cadets had far more enthusiasm for the new course – also, that it is harder to climb ropes in boots than running shoes. They're not going to be climbing ropes in sneakers out on the battlefield.

I think your leadership style changes and morphs over time, but at the core you remain the same.

I am the middle child of nine with an eleven year spread so we are a tight group. I think being a middle child had a significant impact on me. When you are in a big family you need to figure out how to lead and where you fit in.

I had leadership opportunities at a young age – I wanted to be in charge. My older sister often would say I was bossy. If I ran for a student office, I wanted to be the president. If I was on a team, I wanted to be the captain. So I probably was bossy, but I also knew I was a good leader.

The first Women of Wall Street Leadership Boot Camp at West Point, NY.

Postscript:

In the fall of 2013, we had the privilege of having General LeBoeuf (center back row) and Colonel Donna Brazil, (center second row), both representing The Thayer Leadership Development Group, serve as faculty for our Leadership Boot Camp for the Women of Wall Street. The picture above is the group sitting for the class's formal portrait, complete with Army ball caps.

Maureen LeBoeuf
Brigadier General
U.S. Army (Retired)

Hometown
Olean, NY

ST. BONAVENTURE
U N I V E R S I T Y
Founded 1858

1972 – 1976
B.S.
St. Bonaventure University

1976 – 2004
U.S. Army

Leaders create the conditions for others to BE their best.

Defense Advisory Committee
on Women in the Services

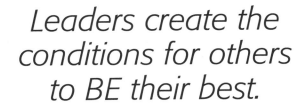

2007

M.S. and Ph.D.
U of Georgia

Duke Sports Medicine
FEAGIN
LEADERSHIP PROGRAM

1997 – 2004
Master of the Sword
U.S. Military Academy

We close with twelve praxes – experiential lessons and skills which you should practice every day to make your leadership, stewardship and decision-making more authentic and aligned.

Parting Praxes

Awake

Start each day with a renewed commitment to be a passionate steward of your leadership role. Leadership is a privilege, not a right. It's a responsibility; it's a way of life, not a title.

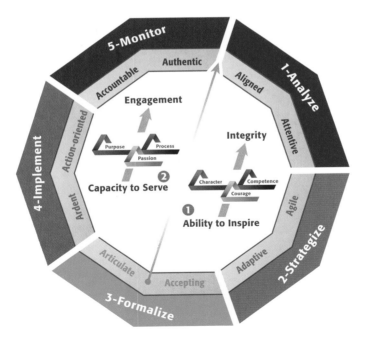

Parting Praxes

Lead Self

The first person you must lead is you. You are responsible for your character, competence and courage – you can't delegate those responsibilities to anyone else, nor can you blame anyone other than yourself when (not if) you fall short. This underscores the importance of the LeaderMetrics® framework, for when you do fail you have a defined path to help you find your way back. This is true even with governance and decision-making. When you skip a Step or Dimension, the process will break down and your sound judgment will be impaired.

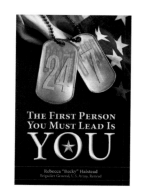

For more on this subject, we would suggest: *24/7: The First Person You Must Lead Is You*, by *Brigadier General Becky Halstead, U.S. Army (Retired).*

3

Love

Be in love with your work and the people that you serve. Love is perhaps the most critical component of leadership, for people can sense when you are coming from a genuine place of love and passion.

Parting Praxes

Stay Strong

We have seen people who have tried to make everyone happy, and in the end they failed as leaders because they lacked the courage to do the right thing at the right time. Also, how you respond to your critics is an important part of your ethos:

Stay positive – trust breaks down when you become defensive and abusive;

Stick to your principles – wavering in front of your critics is like putting blood in shark-infested waters;

Stay away from mud-slinging and retaliation – don't let negativity define who you are; and,

Maintain a sense of humor – "affable" could easily have been our eleventh stewardship attribute.

5

Accept Failure

Don't be afraid of failure, master the art of getting back up (perseverance), and learn how to transcribe what you have discovered through failure to become an even better leader. Our service academies – U.S. Coast Guard Academy in New London, U.S. Military Academy at West Point, U.S. Naval Academy in Annapolis, U.S. Air Force Academy in Colorado Springs, and U.S. Merchant Marine Academy in Kings Point – all have a similar first-year program (freshman year) where Cadets and Midshipmen are subjected to an extremely intense and harsh training environment. There are two reasons for this pedagogy – to see if the Cadet or Midshipman is willing to follow, and whether he or she is able to recover from failure. Before you can be an effective leader you have to learn how to follow, and know how to fail.

Parting Praxes

Give Praise

Always look for ways to reward and praise others for their ideas and contributions. Genuine leaders are not motivated by headlines or receiving credit for work which they did not perform. You'll get greater satisfaction from seeing the spotlight shine on others.

Let Go

As you grow as a leader, you will likely be given more control. Use that opportunity to develop others by delegating more accountability and responsibility.

8

Communicate

Watch how you communicate – your non-verbal, verbal and written communications – and the impact you are having on others. Listening is more important than talking. Lead with your body language and tone. A smile requires 43 muscles, and your followers will be analyzing all 43 each time they see you. If you want followers to be friendly, upbeat and engaged, you have to be friendly, upbeat, and engaged. Prepare your remarks so they are brief and to the point so that your communications are a life ring for your followers who are drowning in information.

Parting Praxes

Be Vigilant

Look for ways to increase your competence – never stop learning and stay current in your professional development. Stay alert for potential problems, and be proactive in seeking resolutions.

Persist

Be persistent in your pursuit of excellence. We are all leaders in training. It is natural to feel that your work is never done, and that there is always something more you can do in the service of others. Persistence builds character, competence and courage, which will give you greater self-confidence in your leadership skills.

Enjoy Life

Maintain a sense of humor, have fun, and make sure you give your followers the space and room to play. Great leaders take breaks and get away, for they recognize that time off is critical for re-energizing, re-focusing and reflecting.

Lead to Serve

Make your work and your life meaningful – lead so that you can be of service to others. Be the point of inspiration for moral, ethical and prudent decision-making.

When you were born, you cried and the world rejoiced.
Live your life so that when you die,
the world cries and you rejoice.

White Elk

Taking Comfort in Leading from the Front

The lawyers and financial experts advised me that the best thing to do was take it through Chapter 11 bankruptcy. However, if we had done that we would have destroyed whatever equity value was left and shareholders would have gotten nothing.

Taking Comfort in Leading from the Front

William F. (Bill) Murdy has been most comfortable leading from the front, whether leading troops in combat or directors in a boardroom. Bill has been the President, CEO and/or Chairman of the Board for four publically traded companies and two large private companies. He knows what it's like to build and lead successful companies, but if you ask him, he'll tell you the crown jewel of his corporate career was leading Comfort Systems USA (NYSE: FIX) out of near bankruptcy.

Bill is a West Point grad – Class of 1964. He was an engineer by academic training, but a combat engineer by choice. He earned "jump wings", the Ranger tab, and the Pathfinder patch. If you're not familiar with Army jargon, it means he would jump out of planes and patrol for weeks in dense jungles and rugged terrain in order to find and establish landing and drop zones for combat missions.

He served two tours in Vietnam and earned a chest full of medals – that are given for heroism, as opposed to the ones you get for being at the right place at the right time. But when you listen to Bill, you learn that his favorite war story and proudest achievement was when he discovered first-hand that sewage does, in fact, flow down hill.

Taking Comfort in Leading from the Front

Bill's unit was deployed to the Dominican Republic in 1965 to intervene in counter-insurgency operations:

I was there with the Army's 82nd Airborne Division as a Lieutenant and platoon leader. The sewer system of Santo Domingo was being used by both the rebels and the loyalists, who we were trying to keep separated. They were using the sewer system right under our positions to pop up and attack us and one another.

That needed to be stopped, so I took a good part of my platoon down into the sewer complex, ultimately mapping the system and setting up barriers and blocking positions while ensuring the continuing flow of sewage.

I remember we waded through that putrid fluid mostly in the dark for a couple of days. I figured it was part of the mission and needed to be done. In the military you don't usually volunteer; there are times enough to get you in trouble just doing the things assigned to you.

Between combat tours and stateside garrison duty, Bill was selected to go the Harvard Business School. "Grad school" is one of the little-known perks that a handful of distinguished junior officers from each of the branches of the armed forces gets to enjoy. For typically a two-year period, junior officers get to let their hair down, settle back into an academic environment and rejoin with society. It's a critical time for officers to recharge their batteries and reconnect with their sense of purpose.

In Bill's case, business school also opened up a path which would lead him away from active duty in the Army and into the corporate world. However, it should be noted that emotionally he never left the Army and to this day he remains one of West Point's most ardent supporters.

Bill's leadership was quickly recognized in the corporate world. He didn't simply progress through increasingly challenging assignments – he hit the ground running – just as he had been trained to do as an airborne ranger. His primary skill was as a turnaround person, helping organizations become more vibrant and productive.

> *"Over my life, I have volunteered to fill leadership positions where I saw something that needed to be done. When no one else was doing it, I just went in and did it and asked permission (or forgiveness) later."*

His biggest challenge would come in 2000 when he was asked to be the Chairman and CEO of Comfort Systems USA, Inc. At the time, Bill was almost 60 years old and could easily have chosen to retire. But he decided otherwise, and accepted the leadership role. As Chairman/CEO, he would have to lead from the front.

Taking Comfort in Leading from the Front

Comfort Systems was, in effect, bankrupt. It had $350 million of current debt, was not cash flow positive and not profitable. The stock had fallen from the high teens to the $1–$2 range.

> *"Comfort was very 'uncomfortable.' I felt like I was back in the sewers in Santo Domingo. The lawyers and financial experts advised me that the best thing to do was take it through Chapter 11 bankruptcy. However, if we had done that we would have destroyed whatever equity value was left and shareholders would have gotten nothing."*

Comfort Systems was a public consolidation (a roll-up) of ninety industrial HVAC (heating ventilation and air conditioning) construction and service companies from around the country. A sizeable portion of the common stock was held by the operators of the companies that had been acquired to form Comfort Systems. They got some cash when they were acquired but took the rest in company stock, so a bankruptcy would have been cataclysmic to the operators.

Bill's first decision was to get in front of the operators – the entrepreneurs and leaders of the acquired firms – to get their commitment to make the overall consolidated company work. He had to communicate a convincing vision and mission, establish values and standards, and reorganize the company without snuffing out the entrepreneurial ethos.

"It was a 24-hour 7-day-a-week job. The synergies of bringing them together had never been exploited."

He pulled the operators together first in regional meetings and later in individual sessions, giving them his commitment and sharing his thoughts. At the time, there was a lot of spending at the corporate headquarters that was seen as unproductive. He knew he had to get the trust of the operating people and one thing he could do was to cut corporate overhead.

Taking Comfort in Leading from the Front

He required corporate leadership to take a 10% pay cut, while he took 20%. He took down a $4 million a year largely outsourced marketing and public relations effort and replaced it with a streamlined, in house, homegrown effort for 1/8 the cost. They got out of the acquisition business, and canceled a planned national meeting of operators. Then he went to work on strengthening the local operating companies and focusing on cash generation.

> *"It was work. It wasn't always fun or pleasant, but I think I was always well-meaning and focused on an end state of creating value for shareholders and employees by creating a sustainable company that efficiently served a need in the market."*

There was some "blood on the floor" but not as much as usual in a turnaround, owing to a commitment to largely re-orient, train and support existing management. The number of operating units was also reduced from ninety to forty-seven.

> *"We were also fighting an economy that was not particularly good, but when 9/11 hit we were strong enough to handle the radical downturn that the economy suffered. A few months later we were strong enough and bold enough to sell off a portion of our operations and pay down the rest of our debt and move into the mid part of the decade to see the company prosper and its stock price move back into the high teens."*

Taking Comfort in Leading from the Front

In May of 2004, while under Bill's leadership, *Barron's* did a story calling Comfort Systems *The Comeback Kid*.

> *You need to know what you are doing to get the trust of your people. You get some trust by demonstrating your competencies; some by demonstrating, on a continuous basis, your character, integrity, honesty and forthrightness. You also earn trust by communicating early and often. And you get trust by involving others in a meaningful way.*

Bill stepped down from being CEO of Comfort Systems at the end of 2012, remaining Chairman until 2014. During his tenure the stock had an annual compounded rate of return of 19% – a feat all the more remarkable considering it was during one of the worst economic recessions in history.

We often see Bill at *The Historic Thayer Hotel at West Point,* which sits on the grounds of the United States Military Academy – The Thayer is where we conduct our Leadership Boot Camps for Investment Stewards. He runs The Thayer much as he has run his other endeavors, by leading from the front. He engages with our participants, faculty and sponsors, and is a point of inspiration –

> *it's what you would expect from someone who's spent his life leading the charge.*

© 2014 Greg E. Mathieson Sr./MAI

William Murdy
Chairman of the Board
Comfort Systems USA
Chairman of the Board,
The Thayer Leader
Development Group

1961 – 1964
U.S. Military Academy

1964 – 1974
U.S. Army

You get trust by involving others in a meaningful way.

1969 – 1970
Harvard Business School

Pacific Resources, Inc.
1974 – 1981
COO

Morgan Stanley

1981 – 1989
Pres/Managing Director
Morgan Stanley Venture
Capital

COMFORT SYSTEMS USA

2000 – 2014
Chairman/CEO/Pres

CLUB QUARTERS®

1999 – 2000
President/CEO

LandCare USA

1997 – 1999
Chairman/CEO

GID

1989 – 1997
Pres/CEO

The Challenge Coin

A challenge coin is a medallion which bears an organization's crest on one side and motto on the other. Traditionally, the challenge coin has been used by elite military units to honor individuals who have gone above and beyond to serve the unit.

Coin designed by Gull Associates (gullassociates.com)

3ethos has carried this tradition over to the leadership development industry. When executives complete training on the LeaderMetrics® framework – which is conducted at West Point in affiliation with *The Thayer Leader Development Group* – participants are awarded their challenge coin at graduation.

People want to be on a team. They want to be part of something bigger than themselves. They want to be in a situation where they feel that they are doing something for the greater good.

"Coach K" (Mike Krzyzewski – USMA '69)

Challenge coin for the Commander, Seventh Coast Guard District (last command for Admiral Branham)

Challenge coin for the Master of the Sword – West Point (last command for General Maureen LeBoeuf)

About the GFS®
(Global Financial Steward) Designation

Preparing leaders to serve more effectively as stewards in critical decision-making roles

The GFS® designation is awarded to professionals who complete an approved course of instruction on *LeaderMetrics*® and pass a comprehensive written final exam.

The GFS® is the first and only professional designation which is based on leadership, stewardship and governance.

About 3ethos and 1920West

3ethos inspires and trains leaders to serve more effectively as stewards in critical decision-making roles.

For more information please visit 3ethos.com

1920West engages and supports coaches and professionals who are passionate about leadership development.

For more information please visit 1920west.com

The Leadership Boot Camp for Investment Stewards is an intensive 2.5-day training program based on the LeaderMetrics® framework, and is conducted in affiliation with *The Thayer Leader Development Group* at West Point.

A tradition with the U.S. Service Academies is to have each class define the motto which will be engraved on their class ring. The Class of 1977 from the U.S. Coast Guard Academy (Don and Admiral Branham are members of the class, and Don serves as the president) has as its motto: *Enter as Many, Leave as One.*

'77 has produced more members of the Senior Executive Service and Admirals, including the current 4-star Commandant of the Coast Guard, Admiral Paul Zukunft, than nearly any other class. Their motto now appears above the doorway of the USCG Academy Alumni Center.

Leaders enable followers to:
Enter as many, leave as one

LeaderMetrics® Self-assessment Instrument

Instructions: This assessment instrument is designed to guide you through a self-examination of your leadership, stewardship and governance/decision-making skills. For each statement, indicate whether it represents one of your strengths (1), one of your weaknesses (4), or an area where you need some improvement (2 or 3).

Leadership Section	Strength (1)		Weakness (4)	
Consider the following statements	1	2	3	4
1 You have the ability to inspire others	O	O	O	O
2 Your behavior is a reflection of your character – what you see is what you get	O	O	O	O
3 You are competent – you are at the top of your profession – you are a lifelong learner	O	O	O	O
4 You are courageous	O	O	O	O
5 Others would say you are a person of integrity	O	O	O	O
6 You work to be of service to others	O	O	O	O
7 You have a sense of purpose – you feel you are responding to a higher calling	O	O	O	O
8 You are passionate about the work you do, and the people you are working with	O	O	O	O
9 You have a defined decision-making process which is consistently applied	O	O	O	O
10 You are effective at engaging others – you have followers	O	O	O	O

Stewardship Section	Strength (1)		Weakness (4)	
Consider the following statements	1	2	3	4
11	ALIGNED: Your work is aligned with your values and principles	○	○	○	○
12	ATTENTIVE: You can anticipate, analyze and prioritize conflicting priorities	○	○	○	○
13	AGILE: You sponsor collaboration	○	○	○	○
14	ADAPTIVE: You deal effectively and quickly with abstract concepts	○	○	○	○
15	ACCEPTING: You value diversity and different worldviews	○	○	○	○
16	ARTICULATE: You are an effective communicator (written and spoken word)	○	○	○	○
17	ARDENT: You are energetic, earnest, and stay on track	○	○	○	○
18	ACTION-ORIENTED: Your followers consider you consistent and reliable	○	○	○	○
19	ACCOUNTABLE: You ensure optimal use of people and resources	○	○	○	○
20	AUTHENTIC: You feel your life is authentic	○	○	○	○

LeaderMetrics® Self-assessment Instrument

	Governance Section		Strength (1)		Weakness (4)	
	Consider the following statements	Dimension	1	2	3	4
21	You have a deliberative process for defining goals and objectives	**1.1**	○	○	○	○
22	You ensure that key decision-makers are aware of their roles and responsibilities	**1.2**	○	○	○	○
23	You ensure that goals and objectives are consistent with applicable regulations, statutes, and established policies and procedures	**1.3**	○	○	○	○
24	RISK: You assess sources and levels of risk when developing a strategy, and ensure key decision-makers are aware of the same	**2.1**	○	○	○	○
25	ASSETS: You consider all your assets – defined ethos, people, unique skills, capital, brands, intellectual property, and physical resources – when developing a strategy	**2.2**	○	○	○	○
26	TIME HORIZON: You identify a time horizon for each goal and objective	**2.3**	○	○	○	○
27	EXPECTED OUTCOMES: You define interim short-term objectives which must be accomplished in order to meet long-term goals and objectives	**2.4**	○	○	○	○
28	You incorporate Risks, Assets, Time Horizon and Expected Outcomes when developing a strategy	**3.1**	○	○	○	○
29	Before formalizing a strategy, you assess whether the strategy can be properly implemented and monitored	**3.2**	○	○	○	○
30	Once you have decided on a strategy, you formally communicate the strategy to key decision-makers and stakeholders	**3.3**	○	○	○	○